DATELINE CHICAGO

DATELINE CHICAGO

A Veteran Newsman
Recalls Its Heyday

WILLIAM T. MOORE
Foreword by Robert Cromie

TAPLINGER PUBLISHING COMPANY · NEW YORK

First Edition

Published in the United States in 1973 by
TAPLINGER PUBLISHING CO., INC.
New York, New York

Published simultaneously in the Dominion of Canada by
Burns & MacEachern Ltd., Ontario

Library of Congress Catalog Card Number: 72-6614

ISBN 0-8008-2114-9

Designed by Jeanette Young

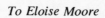

To Eloise Moore

FOREWORD

A longer time ago than it would be polite for you to believe, I was on rewrite for the *Chicago Tribune* with William T. (Bill) Moore, a dapper and talented fellow. Everyone liked and admired him, both because he was so delightful and gentle a man and because he belonged in the uncrowded category of the real pros. It was common knowledge that he, along with many others in the *Tribune* local room, had been a Hearstling; but since he was neat and clean and knew his place, no one minded.

Now this same rewrite man, one of the finest hands with a feature story I've ever come across, has completed his long service with the *Tribune,* a stint that took him to Moscow and Washington, among many other places, and is living the beautiful life in the Florida sun. And he has taken advantage of his unaccustomed leisure (rewrite men and Washington bureau men don't have much of this precious commodity) to turn out a book about his days with the old Chicago *Herald & Examiner.*

It is a book that recreates the "Front Page" era of Chicago journalism—and for any luckless enough not to know, *The*

Front Page is a play written by Ben Hecht and Charles MacArthur, who later wed Helen Hayes, about their experiences in Chicago journalism. It was a time, at least on the *Herald & Examiner* and its sister paper, the Chicago *American,* when gangsters and dance marathons and spicy divorces and all the other flotsam and jetsam of the big city were of more interest than what was happening in the nation's capital or the faraway countries of Europe. Stories were, on occasion, less than truthful; criminals, with astonishing frequency, preferred to surrender to some friendly newsman rather than directly to the law. It was a wacky and engrossing time, a fun time, a time worth reading about.

Moore, who always had a sure eye for the absurd, the touching, the dramatic, and the flamboyant, tells what it was like brushing elbows with Al Capone, Machine Gun Jack McGurn, Big Jim Colosimo, and their henchmen, among whom gangland executions such as the St. Valentine's Day Massacre or the gunning down of Dion O'Banion in his flower shop across from Holy Name cathedral were a commonplace. Despite the years since the Hearst papers have been gone from the building known as "the madhouse on Madison Street," Moore never has forgotten.

Nostalgia is big business now, largely, I suspect, because yesterday seems better than today and few people can bear to think of what tomorrow may become. The occupants of the '20s and '30s may have been crazy, but they enjoyed themselves. Life was brighter (unless of course you happened to be black) and, let's admit it, more livable. The pace was fast, perhaps even faster than it is today. But at the same time it was less wearing and lacked ominous overtones, the sense that the whole world was stumbling toward a doom of such horrible proportions that it doesn't bear thinking about.

There was more laughter, more gaiety, more leisure, paradoxically, since people then worked longer hours. Perhaps the answer is that even as they worked, at least in the newspaper business (formerly known, significantly, as the newspaper game), they were getting a kick out of what they were doing.

Moore's book may leave you with a sense of something missing, something you can't quite put your finger on, that haunts you even as you read. What you are feeling, in my opinion of course, is regret that you no longer find the enjoyment you used to have or, if your generation is a newer one, that you weren't around when the world was merrier, the oddballs more plentiful, and when nobody dreamed of such nightmarish things as the atomic bomb, or that a day was coming when it would be difficult to keep the skies and the waters blue and the animals of the world alive.

But I didn't mean to sound so gloomy a note. This certainly is not a gloomy book. No book could be gloomy with stories in it about Harry Romanoff, the legendary *Her-Ex* police reporter and night editor of the *American,* who mangled the language with such style that he should have been knighted.

"The poison was among the mendicants found in the medicine cabinet," or "The mayor and the governor are at water-logs," or "Don't make a mountain out of a mole," to list a few. Romy ("Don't forget the widows. Get them in there with their widow's tweeds") used to pose as a policeman, a coroner's aide, or anyone else to dig out a story over the phone or in person. But he had one boast: He never wheedled information out of the innocent in a criminal case.

Characters crowd Moore's pages.

Delos Avery, a king among rewrite men, was disturbed by the early-morning noises of the youths in his neighborhood. So he bought a slingshot and began plinking out the windows of nearby houses, knowing the youngsters would be blamed and kept off the streets, thus enabling him to slumber in peace.

The stranger who wandered in one day and was promptly put to work by Abe Geldhof, who thought he was a copyreader seeking employment. But the bewildered visitor, after staring hopelessly at a piece of copy he had been told to rewrite a headline for, finally announced that he was only trying to make a delivery from Walgreen's.

9

The cub reporter, told to do a story on the *Mizpah,* a yacht owned by Eugene McDonald, because: "He's one of our sacred cows." The story the neophyte wrote began: "Commander Eugene McDonald, a sacred cow . . ."

Bill Moore knew them all, including a fellow newsman who spent his entire vacation in a favorite speakeasy, to which his wife brought fresh clothing and whose owner permitted him to use the shower, or Bill Harshe, publicity man for the World's Fair in 1933, who provided shoes for an elephant which, he explained, had tender feet.

The roster of eccentrics is long and lovely: Paddy the Cub, who grew up to avenge the slaying of his father, Paddy the Bear; or the gang that killed the horse that stumbled and threw its rider, Nails Morton, one of the boys, then kicked him fatally in the head.

Too often the good stories and behind-the-scenes information disappear forever because the guys and dolls who knew them delay setting them down until too late.

I'm glad William T. made it.

Robert Cromie

ILLUSTRATIONS

Chicago's Greeter George D. Gaw
Al Capone
Irene Castle McLaughlin
James Hamilton Lewis
Battling Nelson
John Scopes
Eugene McDonald
Sally Rand

following page 160
Chicago Mayor William Hale Thompson
Queen Marie of Rumania
Wilbur Glenn Voliva
Texas Guinan
Bonnie Parker of Bonnie and Clyde
Diamond Louie Alterie and his wife
Louise Rolfe
Smiling Sammie Samoots
St. Valentine's Day Massacre

DATELINE CHICAGO

CHAPTER 1

Managing editor Victor Watson contemplated the lingerie and stockings hung up to dry on the coils above him in William Randolph Hearst's old Chicago *Herald & Examiner*. Those coils were his proudest achievement, his new coffee-making equipment, and any visitor who didn't agree with him that the coffee he poured was better than Lindy's would get a chilly handshake upon his departure.

The lingerie and stockings on his Rube Goldberg invention marred the decor and gave his distilling system a somewhat mawkish look. They had been put there by the bouncing Swedish amazon who was his secretary. She had always done her laundry in the hand basin, and she rejoiced in the metal clothesline that the new managing editor had unwittingly provided for her.

Watson would have enjoyed firing her, to make room for the sexy secretary he had brought with him. She was now cooling her heels as a receptionist, while Watson glowered through his thick glasses and groped for a likely solution to his problems. The owner of the stockings and lingerie, unfortunately, had been left as a legacy to him by his predecessor, who had gone to an even higher post in the Hearst empire, and might therefore be expected to wield an even more potent clout than before. If any hanky-panky were concerned, rejecting the legacy might be a very bad mistake indeed.

There were those in the organization who said Watson was a genius. There were others who said his success was based on the fact that "he knew where the bodies were buried."

But everyone agreed that he had an active and restless mind. It went to work the moment that he realized he could not get rid of his bouncy secretary. He decided to crack down on that wasteful editorial staff. He issued orders that anyone needing a new pencil must come to him personally for it——one pencil at a time.

Then, forgetting his economy drive, he telephoned for eighteen airplanes to fly up and wiggle their wings when Hugo Eckner's Graf Zeppelin arrived for its Chicago visit with Karl Von Wiegand and Lady Hay aboard as Hearst reporters. It cost tremendous money in those days to charter a fleet of airplanes, but Watson reasoned that this was a Hearst promotion and that the savings on pencils would help defray the expense.

Watson reigned in the early Thirties, at the beginning of the end of the fabulous and zany days of the Chicago newspapers —the era portrayed in Charles MacArthur and Ben Hecht's classic *The Front Page*.

The saga of those years, blackened by the Great Depression, bursts the bounds of credulity today. It was an age that is gone, a golden age that somehow vanished. It was an age in which the world hailed Charles A. Lindbergh for flying the Atlantic to Paris and long afterward chuckled admiringly over Wrong Way Corrigan's flight that took him to Ireland because, he said, he started in the wrong direction on his way to the West Coast.

Evangelist Aimee Semple McPherson was lauded for inveighing against sin and Texas Guinan, Queen of the Nightclubs, for encouraging it. Amelia Earhart, the round-the-world flier eventually lost in the Pacific, was the heroine of the skies; and Gertrude Ederle, the conqueror of the English Channel, the heroine of the waters.

Pleasures were simple. With many a whirling windmill, or a tunnel, or a little mechanical goalie with a golf club in his hands as obstacles, we played miniature golf, while the promoters of the miniature golf courses became millionaires. We paid cash rent to sidewalk entrepreneurs for binoculars through which we watched flagpole sitters compete for the longest sit. We went to dance marathons at 2 A.M. to watch Al Capone or Machine Gun Jack McGurn hand out $100 bills to girls who were still hanging on to their partners' necks after days and nights of continuous dancing. Winners of Charleston contests went on to fame on the stage. Bible reading marathons and Paavo Nurmi, the Flying Finn of endurance runners, were the vogue. Six-day bicycle races were as popular as professional football, then struggling for its existence, is now.

The Roaring Twenties and the early Thirties were the era of Prohibition and the speakeasy, where we went upstairs, down into cellars, or to hideouts and waited until a sneaky gangland hanger-on identified us through a peephole in the door. Then we went in to drink an odd thing called a gin buck at ninety-five cents a throw, while we rubbed elbows with policemen who were there either for the fun or because they were part owners of the speak, "had a piece of it," as we put it in our pseudo-sophistication.

Radio was in its awkward, growing years, and television was unborn. And so the big, unexpected news stories were told in extras, special editions published after the regular editions had gone to press. Only the elderly can remember newsboys roaming the streets calling "Extra!" if they were literate, and "Wuxtra!" if they were not.

It was a fabulous era for the news. When millionaires had themselves equipped with monkey glands for one last fling at youth, the papers found out somehow and published the lugubrious facts. The highest-paid reporters were those who could steal diaries from love nests. Next came those who professed familiarity with Al Capone. (They called him Al Brown, as he was known in gangland's inner circles, to prove how close they were to him.)

Gangland's one-way rides, shoot-outs, and bombings were the big news in the Prohibition days, and they left little room for what went on in Washington and the international scene. The Depression went on for years. Nobody gave a hang about foreign relations. Occasionally Washington, but never Moscow or Havana, hit Page One. The news was local murders, society divorces, and Hollywood scandals.

Millionaire heiresses and millionaire playboys scrambled for the glamor, and low pay, of newspaper jobs. Most of them came to work in chauffeur-driven cars at the *Herald & Examiner.* James Weber (Teddy) Lynn, the celebrated University of Chicago English professor, was chairman of the editorial board. A third of our reporters were in society's Blue Book.

Big cities had their official greeters for visiting celebrities. Grover Whelan and his blue shirts and moustache made them welcome in New York, while Greeter George Gaw handed them the keys to the City of Chicago and then went out on his yacht on Lake Michigan to play his steam calliope. The newspapers in New York kept watch on Mayor Jimmy Walker's shipboard farewell parties to make sure they would catch him if he failed to get off on time and found himself headed for Europe with a hangover and, hopefully, a dame.

When the Dionne quintuplets were born, wondering millions got it from the newspapers, not from television flashes, just as they had when Teddy Roosevelt and his Rough Riders stormed Kettle Hill at San Juan. When Big Tim Murphy was gangland's victim in an ambush, and when Al Capone was sent to prison, it was the newspaper extras that brought the tidings.

Murder mysteries fascinated the readers, and the reporters, not the police, solved them. When the police had dug perilously near to China without discovering the body, the star reporter dug it up from beneath the proper mulberry bush, hauled it away to the managing editor's office, and then, after the final edition had gone to press with the exclusive story, called in the police, gave them the corpse, and told them what had happened.

The deathwatch was automatic. If a mayor, a banker, or a gangster was dying, the reporters lined up in twenty-four-hour shifts outside the hospital, awaiting the pull of a blind or some other signal from the physicians that the man was dead.

It was a wondrous age. F. Scott Fitzgerald performed his literary miracles. Jimmy Sheehan's stories produced *The Desert Song*. "Rose Marie" had the nation weeping. Sally Rand, a generation ahead of her time, introduced the nation to nudity, scarcely concealed by her celebrated fans. Wilbur Glenn Voliva exhorted his followers against the sin of eating oysters and taught them that the world is flat. Irene Castle, long past her dancing years, fought against the vivisection of dogs.

Everyone who was anyone had his own private railroad car. Samuel Insull was God. A financial writer doubted it but lacked the nerve to express his doubts. He was fired for not reporting the impending collapse of the Insull utilities empire—after the empire had collapsed.

Watson's arrival from New York was an epic performance. He came to town in a chauffeur-driven limousine bearing New York license plate No. 1, in the days when No. 1 was reserved for state governors. He scanned the day's final edition of the paper he had come to boss and came upon a paragraph that fascinated him. It was one I had written about a fake preacher who ran a religious cult and chased the little girls of his congregation. He had been arrested on the children's accusations, and the judge had ordered him to take a psychiatric examination.

I had written that the judge had decreed a sanity test for the self-styled Celestial Messenger, but "sanity" got into the paper as "sanitary." Without consulting his editors, Watson had gone down to the composing room and had a bulletin set up in type and printed. It quoted the paragraph I had written and said: "The man who wrote this has been fired."

Nobody had fired me, and the first inkling I had of the trouble I was in came when the day city editor, Jack McPhaul, called my attention to the message on the bulletin board. City editor Harry Canfield dug up my original copy, which showed that the mistake had not been mine, and I was reinstated without ever having been fired. Life with Watson was like that.

The *Herald & Examiner* editors always fascinated me. Forty thousand dollars a year was high pay for managing editors in those days. The paper never was a money maker, but Mr. Hearst's vanity required that he maintain two papers in such cities as Chicago and New York. And he had a penchant for getting promising men under contract, whether he had a job for them or not.

And so there was generally a working managing editor, as well as a reserve managing editor, waiting for the day when the working editor would stub his toe. The reserve man had a cubbyhole for an office. The working managing editor had something surpassing a movie set, albeit, in Watson's case, it could be somewhat marred by a Swedish secretary and her lingerie.

Charles Stanton, who left her as his legacy to Watson, was one of those who had made it to the managing editor's office by the cubbyhole route. He was a distinguished-looking, tall, white-haired man, wise enough to leave the running of the paper to astute subordinates who knew how. Late in the evening he would come in white tie from the opera or the theater to see how things were getting along and then go home.

His reign was at the time of the Robert Elliott Burns book *I Was a Fugitive from a Georgia Chain Gang*. One day a gaunt man with a rough exterior and a hungry look talked his way past the one-armed doorman and got into the city room. His story was brief, and painful. He, too, he said, was a fugitive from a chain gang, in desperate fear of being captured. Could he just live in the city room? The prison authorities, he assured us, were outside waiting for him. He pointed them out to us on street corners, although we had no way of knowing whether they were speakeasy bartenders or prison guards.

Stanton didn't really believe the man's story, but, being a very compassionate fellow, he turned over his private shower to him and began bringing him fresh clothes. The staff brought our visitor more and gave the copyboys money to buy him sandwiches downstairs at DeMet's. The professed fugitive stayed in the city room for weeks, perhaps to dodge an estranged wife who was suing him for alimony, and we never did find out the truth of the matter. He just disappeared one night.

Ash De Witt was the current day managing editor, a cut below the managing editor. Mr. Hearst had gone to Europe and fallen in love with English papers. Upon his return, he decreed that the *Her-Ex* should inaugurate a British page. De Witt called on me to write it.

Thereafter, while the British page lasted, I wrote the strangest stories of my career. They were based upon the deadly accounts the City News Bureau gathered from the police stations for all the Chicago newspapers, but the sergeants who wrote the blotters and the British never would have recognized them. I set the stage in the first paragraph with something like this:

An odd thing happened last night in a flat at 1237 Chelsea Street. Elmer Johnson, Esquire, went to bed dreaming of hominy grits after a bit of a tiff with his wife, who had refused to cook them on the grounds that he had spent too much time in the neighborhood pub.

Johnson, a greengrocer who weighs sixteen stone, muttered something in his sleep about a girl he had met in the pub. His wife decided to cook the grits after all.

She put them in her biggest pot and poured them, boiling water and all, over the face of her sleeping spouse.

Then she called the bobbies, who arrested her on a charge of suspicion of the improper use of hominy grits and attempted murder.

Eventually I got rid of the British-page assignment in a very odd way: a husband-and-wife fight. The editor who had assigned me to it had gone some place else in the Hearst organization, and I had a new day managing editor. The *Her-Ex* was strictly a one-cabin paper, where copyboys would call the editors by their first names. I was not surprised, therefore, when my new day managing editor told me he was taking his wife to the six-day bicycle races and invited me and my wife to go along.

It began as a wondrous evening. To that long-forgotten spectacle society came around midnight from the opera, the theater, and the gay parties the smart set attended in burlesque houses. The Capones, the prizefighters, and all the notables of the sporting world also came. The political figures never missed. And so we watched admiringly as the racers spun about the track endlessly, until the time came for us to go home.

We were about to step through the door when the managing editor caught sight of a newsboy and stopped to buy the latest editions of the *Her-Ex* and the *Tribune,* to assure himself we hadn't been scooped. Our wives, unaware of the delay, walked out and the door closed behind them. My boss took a quick look at the front pages of both papers and then looked around for the ladies.

I told him I thought they were outside, but he insisted that they were within, powdering their noses. We waited and waited and waited, because he was certain they hadn't left, and he was a man you didn't cross. Finally I slipped out, and there they were, unable to get back in without buying tickets, and the boss's wife had flatly refused to buy them or to let Eloise do it.

The boss gave his wife a tongue-lashing for keeping him waiting and she responded in kind, each blaming the other for the slight mix-up they were blowing up into a *cause célèbre.*

Meanwhile, smartly dressed folk who might have recognized all of us were streaming past, and I tried to get our warring friends out of the picture.

It was in vain. He was a tremendous man, and she was big and formidable. Both were the soul of dignity under normal circumstances. But suddenly they lapsed into accusations that must have been part of every fight they ever had.

"Shame on Benjie! Shame on Benjie!" she began to scream.

Drawing himself up in all his husbandly dignity, he screamed right back: "Shame on Benjie? No. Shame on Gracie!"

The fascinated crowd about us was growing larger, but there they stood in the lobby, yelling, "Shame on Gracie? No. Shame on Benjie!" and vice versa. The row seemed longer than the six days and nights of the bicycle races.

Then he caught sight of a Yellow Cab that had stopped in front of the stadium. Out he dashed, with his good wife in hot pursuit. The driver flung the door open, but it was too late. She hurled herself upon Benjie from the rear and held him, explaining to Eloise and me, as we caught up with them, "He isn't going to get away with this."

We waved the cabdriver away and went to Benjie's car, with our host and hostess still doing their "shame on" act. Silence closed in and they drove us home. Nobody spoke.

The following morning he strode past the tiny glass compartment that was my office in the city room, without looking in, and went to his own compartment office, whence he telephoned me. We could see each other as he told me tersely, "I have canceled the British page. You're back working for the city editor. Report to him for assignment."

No longer a specialist, I had to give up my glass compartment and move back to my old desk in the rewrite battery. Seven weeks passed. Benjie never even spoke to me or came near me. Then one day he came over and slapped me warmly on the back. Assuming the pose of a benevolent and forgiving monarch, he said, "I began speaking to my wife again today."

The glass compartments, strange for a vast, wide-open city room, were a saga in themselves. The first act of a new managing editor, if he were any respecter of *Her-Ex* tradition, was to order some installed if there weren't any, or order them removed if they were already in existence.

The patient but astute building maintenance men were fully aware of this quirk of managing editors. If they were ordered to destroy the glass enclosures, they merely took them down to the basement and stored them. Thus, when a new managing editor ordered glass enclosures built for all the editors who didn't have offices and for the specialists, all the maintenance crew had to do was to get the glass panels out of mothballs and put them up.

CHAPTER 2

There were fabulous sights to be seen in the city room, and the most incredible of all was Romy, who had been christened Harry Romanoff. He was a short, roly-poly man who had been gazing enchanted upon a glittering and unbelievable world for years, a grown-up brownie in the guise of a tough police reporter, wearing his heart upon his sleeve.

He had ready tears for the mailman sent to jail for stealing a doll for his invalid daughter and welling indignation for the frail little old woman whose grandson butchered her. His voice trembled when he reported the death of the old-time harness horse trainer who expired believing that his driver was sending his latest horse to victory. Every minute of the day was a crisis to Romy.

He was the *Her-Ex*. The staff cursed the loud-mouthed, scheming poseur of the city room—and went through hell for him when he asked it. He was the paper's shot in the arm, a dynamic police reporter with the authority of an editor. He never left the office and did all his work by telephone. He knew every corner drugstore in Chicago and hence could summon the police by phoning the store nearest to the scene of a crime and cajoling the druggist into going a-running for the nearest policeman.

This sentimental wizard could be as tough as he was soft. Romy threatened police captains: "You goddamn whorehouse pimp, come clean with me or I'll have you pounding pavements in Hegewich. Where's the body?" He flattered telephone operators into superhuman accomplishments: "Listen, Lovely, you're a thousand miles away from me, and if you say you can't get that sheriff for me I know you can't. But I know you can do it, and you will do it, too, for a tired old man."

He flattered big business men who had guilty consciences: "Mr. Pomeroy, this is one of the biggest bankers in Chicago. You can understand why I don't dare mention my name on the telephone, with you 'way up there in Michigan, but you know me and I know you. We both want to catch the Yellow Kid, and I think he's who we're after.

"I got taken the same way, you see. I just called to ask you how he got your wife to give him the $60,000. It'll be just between you and I and the gatepost. Teensy-weensy. Tête-à-tête.

"She was in bed, was she? Confidentially, he was staying there while you were up to the lake with this Margie? Oh, I just happened to know. We'll never mention Margie again . . . Honor bright.

"Now that's all I wanted to know. That lets I and the detectives know how to go after this rascal confidence man. All right, old boy. All right, Len. All right, Lennie. Goodbye, Lennie Kid. And now if any of those newspaper folks call you, don't say a word. It might G-string our investigation, see?"

In those days, there were shrewd but wrong gentlemen who wondered for years how their innermost thoughts turned up on

Page One. They talked to no one save a certain Birger of the deputy's office, or a banker of such importance that he couldn't even whisper his name over the telephone. And the gentlemen who called obviously didn't betray them, for the callers to a man warned them particularly, before hanging up, not to talk to reporters.

Romy always pretended he told the people he interviewed to refuse to speak with reporters so as to keep rival papers from getting the story. That figured in it, of course. But Romy's overriding purpose was to impress the listening staff with one last masterstroke. His methods were devious, but his principles were strong. He never wheedled information out of the innocent. You had to be wrong, very wrong, to get the Romy treatment.

He had three telephones working a moment after the flash came on a big story, unless it were one of the many bombings of the Prohibition era. But in those boisterous days of gangland, bombing stories had to wait for Romy's song. Over the telephone would come the bulletin. Solemnly, Romy would silence the office with three mighty blows of his metal printer's rule on his swinging brass lampshade. Then, gleefully, he would sing out in his stentorian voice:

"She-caw-go! She-caw-go! Boom! Boom! Boom!"

The smile would vanish from his face and he would be after the story by telephone, never to rest until the last word had been hammered out on a rewrite man's typewriter. With his knowledge of the locations of the drugstores, he could always contact a policeman at the scene to tell what had happened before the outside reporters could even get there. His was the most tremendous, the most bewildering concentration of energy I have ever seen.

Every story was a trifle more important, more crucial, than the last. A paragraph or five columns, it was all the same to Romy—amazing, the greatest story since the dawn of civilization. Let great newspapermen pride themselves on keeping their voices deadly calm at such moments; Romy enjoyed bellowing and he had the voice for it.

He approached each story with the open-mouthed wonder of a child. Once he had gathered his information, he would sit down beside the rewrite man and in his excitement shout the facts until the details could be distinctly heard in the faraway sports department. Astute city editors stood beside him, imploring him at intervals to try to lower his voice lest he burst the rewrite man's eardrums or begging him to stop in time for the rewriter to catch the edition with the major facts. But one by one Romy blasted the editors out of his way with his swelling roar. At the end, only he would be in there, unmuzzled and unbowed.

Romy, who died at seventy-nine, just after the Chicago Press Veterans had elected him Press Veteran of the Year, in 1970, never minimized a story. That was blasphemy. "They heard the rat-a-tat-tat of machine guns," he would say, "and four of the Moran gang fell dead." "You mean the killers used machine guns?" the suspicious rewrite man would demand. Trapped, Romy still wouldn't give up the hope that the rewriter would fall for his implication even then. He was enthusiastic, but honest. "Well," he would confess, "I guess nobody actually saw the machine guns, but everyone heard the rat-a-tat-tat." Oftener than not, the guns turned out to be revolvers.

Because he was a voracious reader, and an opera and theater fan, we never could decide whether his hilarious language was an affectation or a reversion to words and phrases he had picked up as a child. On short stories he was forever calling for a paragraph and a half. I've never yet figured out how to write half a paragraph.

Romanisms we called Mr. Malaprop's expressions, of which his most notable was his final admonition to the rewrite men after every gangland shooting: "And don't forget the widows. Get them in there in their widow's tweeds."

Other celebrated Romanisms were:

If you don't want to write the story, forget it; it's only mandatory. . . . The poison was among the mendicants found in the medicine cabinet. . . . Tell 'em the punishment the law metted out in the first paragraph. . . . He's gone hogwire. . . . The mayor and the governor are at waterlogs. . . . The sheriff's trying to G-string the investigation. . . . They've thrown down the cudgel to us. . . . It happened in the wee little small hours. . . . If the story's too long we'll get the copy desk to eke out a couple of paragraphs.

The list was endless: Just write the gist of it (hard G). . . . It's only a gesture (hard G). . . . Make the weather man explain the humidity; ask him how many humids there are. . . . The story's only a grain of salt. . . . Let's cut out all these old platitudes and get some new ones into our stories. . . . The doc can't lie on the witness stand because of his hypocritical oath. . . . Let's show 'em something new—write a good smash-bang trite story. . . . The robbers got approximately $23,571.09. . . . Don't make a mountain out of a mole.

Romy's masterpiece was coined to protect the staff during the visits of the Hearst efficiency experts, whom we called the Wrecking Crew. The crew was out to eliminate unnecessary employees, and so Romy would go among the reporters on the occasion of each visitation, issuing this solemn warning: "Don't congregate in groups!"

He could play, too, as the late editor of the New York *Journal-American* Seymour Berkson discovered when he was a fledgling *Her-Ex* reporter. Berkson had misgivings the day he went to the railroad station to take a train to California, for Romy had sent him off on his vacation with a peculiar gleam in the Romanoff eye. Berkson knew he was getting the works à la Romanoff when the conductor tapped him on the shoulder and asked him to step out onto the observation platform. So does a gangster when he is inviting you to take a one-way ride, but it's no good resisting. With his knees buckling beneath him, Berkson faltered out to the platform, followed by several passengers.

"Hi, Prince!" he heard. "Right over here, your Highness." And a dozen *Her-Ex* flashlight guns boomed. (Camera flashlights in those days were long tubes of powder, twice as powerful as gunpowder. The powder was lighted and then held aloft on a long pole. The resultant explosion frequently singed the beard or hair of the mayor or other dignitary who was being photographed. I still bat my eyes when my picture is taken by flashlight, as a result of a singeing I got when I arrived late at a party thrown by Chris Paschen. My picture, with my eyes shut and my hair afire, hung for years in Chicago's Brevoort Hotel, where Chris served champagne—in Prohibition days. I looked like a zombie.)

Berkson did what any gentleman going for a one-way ride would do. He ran, to hide at the other end of the train. But it was too late. All the way to the coast he was pointed out as a prince, a real prince, traveling incognito. Mothers trapped him into conversations with their gangling daughters, and then slipped delightedly away. Everyone wanted to know who he really was. When he told them that he was just a *Her-Ex* cub reporter on vacation, the passengers only shook their heads and replied sagely that they understood. But they promised him the secret would be safe with them if he'd only tell them who he really was.

Feeling particularly clownish one day, Romy identified himself as General Sole when he telephoned to New York to ask for some confidential information from a pompous malefactor. The victim of the hoax was unaware that in some army circles General Sole was a designation for a soldier who is S.O.L., or, in the parlor version, slightly out of luck. Flattered out of his shoes by a call from a general, the gentleman gave Romy information that wild horses could not have dragged from him.

One wild Romanoff was the equal of 242 wild horses, or 187 wild hippopotami. Recognizing this, the waggish editors publicized him sometimes in half-page advertisements filled with the exploits of the reporter who never left the office. The other half of the page was a plug for the amazing stories the *Her-Ex* published about strange lands and creatures. The illustration for the latter was a hippo almost as big as the photo of Romy. He used to beg them to keep the hippo out, because all his friends seemed to think there was a likeness.

Delos Avery, the true gentleman of the rewrite staff (he was a Harvard man who indignantly denied it), enjoyed flea circuses and chess. He found a combination of the two irresistible. One entire vacation he spent in New York, playing chess with the owner of a flea circus.

Although the accepted procedure for sending copy to the city desk in those days before copygirls was to yell "Boy!" and hand it to the first copyboy who responded, Avery found the system too boring. He went downstairs to Walgreen's drugstore and bought himself a mechanical toy caterpillar tank. Thereafter, even on a deadline, he wound up his mechanical wonder, put in his copy, aimed at the city desk, and sent it inching on its way. The harried editor in the slot, knowing that he couldn't win against Avery, would wind up the tank and send it back for more copy. But even this palled on Avery. Eventually, he set up an obstacle course by placing telephone books along the route. He always was overjoyed when the sturdy little tank rumbled triumphantly over them.

Avery, a dour old bachelor, was a relentless bubble burster, and so he looked with a jaundiced eye on the story that Pete Genna of the celebrated Genna gang was having visitations from the Blessed Virgin. Every night, hundreds who gathered outside his house were willing to swear, she appeared on the wall of an adjacent building for all to see. Her shadow was fifteen feet high.

31

Those who knew the Gennas said that one of the family had long ago stolen the jewels of the Madonna from an ancient cathedral in their native Italy and that the shadow had come to haunt Pete and his family. The devout fell to their knees in the street; the skeptics sneaked around to see if the reports of the miracle were true and found to their disappointment that everything was just as the newspapers had reported.

And then one night someone in the Genna household chanced to pull down a shade. It cut off the reflection from a statue in the home that had been projected in heroic size by a lamp. And the miracle of the Blessed Virgin, Avery gleefully wrote, was explained.

Avery investigated the miracle of the filling station whose owner had brought in a gusher oil well. The oil was so bountiful that it came right up through the floor of the station, puzzling the station owner as much as it delighted him. He couldn't decide whether to sell stock or keep the whole oil well for himself until Avery went out personally and discovered that the oil was coming from a leak in the tank.

The only miracle he ever recognized was performed by Romy. Avery's pocket was picked for an even hundred dollars when a hundred dollars was still money. Romy telephoned the attorney whose business was to get out writs to spring the dips in case they didn't report by telephone every two hours, because that meant they had been arrested. Unless the money was back in twenty-four hours, Romy warned, the heat would be turned on the pickpockets' organization. Next morning the money, in Avery's wallet, was brought in by a messenger who said his boss had found it.

One of the rules of Avery's life was to conserve his energy for matters of importance, his hobbies. Given a mailbag of letters from one of the readers' contests the *Her-Ex* was forever running, and told that he must pick the day's three winners, he approached the task with utmost calm. Half an hour later, another mailbag was brought in.

"Here are some more letters for you, Delos," the city editor called out.

"Keep 'em," Avery replied impartially. "The first three on the top of the other batch were good enough for me."

He always denied the Midget Ferneckes story, but it was told to me on the highest authority. Midget was the top blower of bank safes in the Middle West, and also Number I in escapes from the penitentiary. He was at the time at liberty, via the escape route.

Avery was a scholar and a perfectionist. He set out to be a master in each field that attracted him. Deciding, in late middle age, to become a golfer, he bought an assortment of clubs, sweaters, caps, and plus fours, which were then having a heyday among the well-dressed golfers. He hired a professional to teach him the game and practiced interminably, getting up at dawn to be on the course. In time he became so proficient that he won a municipal golf tournament. Victory achieved, he promptly lost interest in the game. He brought all his equipment and fancy clothes to the office and let the staff members take their pick. And he never played another round. Besides, it interfered with his slingshot practice. Avery was a late sleeper who objected to the noise boys made beneath his window. So he went down to Von Lengercke & Antoine and bought a foreign-made slingshot. Then he shot out windows in the neighborhood. The noisy boys were blamed, and Avery could sleep as long as he wished.

It was the same with motoring. When he decided to learn to drive, this gentleman who went everyplace in taxicabs bought himself the sportiest car he could find. His instructors despaired of ever teaching him the intricacies of his mechanical monster, but he was determined. He reached the point at which he could drive through the slim Sunday-morning traffic to Chicago's Loop. Skimming faultlessly through it for a few Sundays, he acknowledged himself to be a master, turned his car in, and went back to taxis.

33

And so he was following his natural inclinations when he bumped into Midget Ferneckes, safe blower par excellence, at the John Crerar Library. Avery, who wouldn't have harmed a fly, had become fascinated by the Borgias. He wanted to duplicate the poisons with which they killed their enemies. There was another researcher at the table where Avery worked—Midget Ferneckes. He was a perfectionist, too. Despite his awesome reputation as a safe blower, he had come to bone up on explosives, in the one place the police would never look for him.

At the reading table, day by day, the researchers became acquainted. Avery studied the wig and the obviously false moustache. He began wondering what the little man would look like without them. And then it dawned on him: The little man would look like the pictures the papers had printed of Midget Ferneckes.

A million dollars, it was estimated, Midget had cached when he finally found himself in the penitentiary after he had made two attempts to bomb his way out of the county jail. It was years later that a tiny man in black glasses approached the interview clerk in Joliet penitentiary one sultry afternoon and handed him a slip of paper that read "Amenn, 4408." That was the name and number of a prisoner who had been transferred some time before to the new Illinois prison at Stateville.

The Midget, posing as a visitor from outside the walls, said he wished to visit his friend, Amenn. The clerk directed the prisoner to the new penitentiary, nearby, and pushed the buzzer to let the guard know it was all right to permit the visitor to pass. So Midget Ferneckes walked out a free man, after all those years, in his black glasses and the prison clothes he had dyed. When they caught him in Chicago near the John Crerar Library, they searched him, for they knew him of old, and then searched him again. It wasn't until the next morning that they found the secret pocket they were looking for. It was too late, then, for Midget had killed himself with the poison he kept in it in case he was rearrested.

CHAPTER 3

Flamboyant Victor Watson was a vain man and he was the original hard-luck editor when his vanity was concerned. He arrived just in time for Chicago's Century of Progress Exposition of 1933 and 1934. In a brief survey of Chicago, which he regarded as his personal domain, he decided the city had placed its statue of Garibaldi in the wrong place. He approved of Sally Rand, the fan dancer who established her fame at the World's Fair, but disapproved of the fair's management and of Mayor Edward J. Kelly. Chicago's Loop, he proclaimed, should be made Parisian, with sidewalk cafés.

The mayor took to the radio to denounce Watson as a carpetbagger from New York. The fair management resented the criticism of this stocky little man who always wore a belted-all-around coat. The restaurateurs rose in arms against the edict that they serve on the sidewalk, but, miraculously, some of them went along. But, a born loser, Watson had to watch in agony as his sidewalk cafés went down the drain. They couldn't last in

Chicago's lusty climate in the days when ropes had to be strung along stately Michigan Boulevard to keep pedestrians from being blown from the sidewalks into motor traffic.

One of his earliest promotions was of young Ida Jean Kaine, the beauty writer. He gave her the same treatment that he accorded the movie star Marion Davies, Mr. Hearst's favorite, when one of Miss Davies' pictures opened in Chicago. The build-up for Ida Jean was tremendous, but on the day her column began, Watson couldn't even get the title printed correctly in his own paper. It was to have been "Your Figure, Madame," but it came out "Madame, Your Figure." He gave a hotel luncheon for VIP's to launch the column, but the paper got the hour wrong and a number of guests arrived late.

Frustrated on every front, Watson decided to make the city courteous. He had heard that passengers sometimes got jostled on the elevated trains and that sales persons in stores were rude. And so, with a wave of his magic wand, he transformed radio reporter Steve Healy into the *Her-Ex*'s courtesy reporter and sent him out each day to award prizes to the courteous. The prizes were doubled in case the courteous persons were also tactful, i.e., carrying a copy of the *Her-Ex* when Healy tapped them on the shoulder. In addition to making Chicago courteous, wily Watson hoped to increase circulation. Only a dope, he reasoned, would venture out without a copy of the *Her-Ex* under his arm.

Each evening, Healy recounted his experiences of the day on the *Her-Ex* radio station and announced the winners. So it was with pleasant anticipation that Watson rubbed his hands as he sat in his luxurious apartment with a top government official from Washington, waiting for Healy to come on the air. Watson had summoned me to write a story on his guest's reaction. It was a rather thick-voiced courtesy reporter who broke the silence at last—a minute and a half late.

"Folksh," he said, "I'm tired of handing you thish guff every night. I didn't see a courteous gal or guy all day. And I didn't meet anyone with a *Herald & Examiner*."

The paper had always abounded in mental giants and stuffed shirts. No one ever knew which was which. A new managing editor from out of town might choose a second-string police reporter for his confidential advisor or pick one from a group of strangers sitting in the reception room hoping to get a job. There was always a fair-haired boy who had the managing editor's confidence.

And so it came as no surprise when Watson picked his first fair-haired boy from outside the newspaper game, a jobless fellow who had haunted the reception room for three days. The managing editor at first wouldn't see him. Then one day the future big shot caught Watson coming in, buttonholed him, and told him what was wrong with the city government.

Watson was charmed, enchanted. The next day the jobless stranger was his political advisor and confidant. Within a few weeks the stranger was advising the chiefs of the advertising department how to sell their advertising and showing the rewrite men a few tricks in writing stories. He came to work in a chauffeur-driven car.

Another of Watson's confidential advisors on policy was a gnomelike little man with a pleasant though dazed smile who skipped into the office with that sprightliness that some men get in their late seventies. Half a minute after he had sent his name in he was in Watson's office. A reporter who chanced to wander past the open door was presently whispering in the ear of everyone in the city room that the stranger must be a brother-in-law of Mr. Hearst, judging by the affectionate way in which the visitor and Watson had embraced.

Next day the bouncing little old man was ensconced at a desk in the managing editor's office. Ever smiling his bewildered smile, which we were now beginning to suspect was really one of disarming shrewdness, he popped in and out with strange ideas, some good, some bad, for the editors. That was the way, however, that all managing editors' ideas were, and we carried these out without question, even though we feared one of the worst ones might one day wreck the paper. Certainly we had no reason to question the advisability of what the little old man told us to do, since he obviously had the sanction of the managing editor.

Sometimes our eccentric septuagenarian wrote news stories, which the editors published without changing a word. Sometimes he wrote blazing editorials in the manner of Arthur Brisbane. Frequently he wrote poems and got them printed. On occasion, pretty girls of the staff complained that he had pinched them, but it was generally agreed that he might be pardoned an occasional pinch on grounds of age, a frolicsome nature, and his exalted position as friend and confidant of the managing editor.

When he moved on, eventually, to heckle the staff of some other paper, we put him down as another lugubrious experience of working for the *Her-Ex*. It was by the merest chance that we ever heard of him again. Some thrifty reporter who had saved enough money for a trip to New York, instead of shooting it at the speakeasy across the street, ran into a New York reporter who knew the old codger's story.

He had been an inconsequential figure who answered telephones on the city desk of one of Mr. Hearst's Manhattan papers. When he had outlived his usefulness, Mr. Hearst, who saw even the sparrows fall in his organization, sent out a message to all his managing editors asking if one of them could find a spot for the superannuated gentleman. Our boss generously volunteered, aware, doubtless, that his generosity would get him a gold star in Mr. Hearst's book.

Having no work for the goldbrick he had bought with his eyes open, Watson gave him the run of the office and certainly never knew of the strange orders thereafter issued in the managing editor's name. The old fellow had never had any more authority than a copyboy; until he came to the *Her-Ex* he never expected to have any. But when he discovered that he had been clothed with some magic power beyond his ken, he went wild with it, bossing everyone on the paper except the managing editor himself. So went the *Her-Ex*.

Watson, for all his title, never was supreme after the advent

39

of Fred Eldridge, a veteran of the early days of the Hearst empire. Eldridge worked without a coat, in bright blue shirts and Herbert Hoover starched collars, and had an old man's predilection for several old maid reporters who worked in the suburbs. He came to the paper as supervising editor for it and a half dozen other papers in the chain. He really ran the show as its supervising managing editor.

He was an ancient, unsmiling editor with a curled lip and a heart that wasn't pure gold. The staff alternated between calling him Dracula and the Smiling Lieutenant, for he was a dour fellow.

Well aware that he had to get along with Eldridge, Watson issued a statement, when he learned about the Dracula and Smiling Lieutenant business, that Eldridge had a heart as big as Lake Michigan. When you got to know him, Watson added thoughtfully. Eldridge promptly demonstrated what Watson meant by suspending an impoverished copyreader for two weeks without pay for a trifling error.

Everyone below the managing editor fraternized with the staff on the *Her-Ex,* and sometimes even Watson did. It was a timid copyboy indeed who knew anyone as Mister. Yet the managing editor, any managing editor, was a man of complex mentality and devious methods. He puttered around making coffee or conjuring up health methods for the staff or experimenting with chain letters to see if he really could fall into half a million dollars. If he had an idea, he wrinkled his forehead and chopped it out in half a dozen vague words that only puzzled the editors under him. And they, for their part, never asked him to elaborate, lest he think them slow to comprehend. Instead, they nodded sagely, giving him the impression that he had indeed expressed himself with clarity and force.

Then they hurried out to huddle and ask one another if anyone had any idea what the Old Man meant. If they seldom approximated his thought, they never knew the difference, for the managing editor would have forgotten and proceeded to cook up something infinitely vaguer by the time they had carried out what they thought were his orders. The paper could have been revolutionized, and shorn of its quaint charm in the process, had any of the yes-men ventured just once to tell the ·mastermind: "I didn't quite get that one, Sire. Would you mind keeping them on the ground?"

CHAPTER 4

The soul of decorum was white-haired Charles Stanton when he was managing editor. He believed his employees and his paper should have dignity. Since he did not spend much time in the office, he did not recognize the photographer he met on alighting from a train but did note the name of the *Her-Ex* on the photographer's camera bag. Ever anxious to learn more about his paper, Stanton engaged the fellow in conversation, to insure himself that the dignity of the *Her-Ex* was being maintained.

"What kind of pictures are you after, my boy?" the symbol of propriety asked.

"Movie actresses, Bud," the irreverent photog replied. "Legs! That's what the *Herald & Examiner* likes: legs."

Stanton was the only one of our long succession of bosses who ever tried to do anything about the early editions, copy paper, and stories that hadn't pleased their authors which always littered the city room floor ankle deep, and sometimes knee deep. He solemnly pledged himself to get us all new metal desks if we would stop using the floor for a wastebasket for a year. In eager, childish glee, a staff accustomed to battered old wooden desks from the turn of the century took him up. We would have torn early editions to shreds and eaten them in preference to letting them fall from our desks, so eager were we to get that modern furniture of steel. We got a new managing editor instead. When I left, the *Her-Ex* was still using the old wooden desks that threatened to fold up without warning.

The new desk proffer was typical of the measures that editors took to keep the staff happy. They seemed to regard such improvements as infinitely more attractive to the reporters than better pay, and the peculiar thing about it was that the editors were so often right. When I decided to resign after thirteen years of service, managing editor Johnnie Dienhart mumbled something about more money in a desultory sort of way and then changed the subject before I could catch him up on it. He pointed to the workmen who were as usual hammering aimlessly upon some pipes.

"My God," he exclaimed paternally, a shining light in his eye. "Do you know what that is? Air conditioning! You're walking out on $100,000 worth of air conditioning."

It wasn't air conditioning. The workmen were pounding on the pipes because something had gone wrong with the air pressure tubes that brought copy across the Loop underground from the City News Bureau. Johnnie nevertheless had no intention of deceiving me. He just thought that air conditioning would appeal to him if he were leaving a paper that had never had it, and so he willed it that it was air conditioning that had brought the workmen there.

Johnnie, who had almost become a druggist instead of a member of the Fourth Estate, was as interested in home remedies as in gadgets, and he saw no reason why a good home remedy man could not apply his homely methods to a business building. Here he could carry on an employees' health service of his own in his odd moments, independent of the company physicians. In wintertime, therefore, he attached funnels to the valves of radiators, opened the valves, and then tiptoed happily around dropping eucalyptus oil and other mendicants, as Romy called them, into the funnels. We lived as a result in a continuous fog, pungently scented, and marveled that Johnnie himself so often had the sniffles.

We all loved Johnnie, and so he was not included in the list of editors in the slogan the news staff recommended in 1935. Mindful of the slogan that captured the nation for Hearst's *American Weekly,* "The Nation's Reading Habit," the *Her-Ex* conducted a staff contest to discover a slogan for the paper in 1936.

The almost unanimous choice of the editorial department was: "More Pricks in Thirty-Six."

The copydesk, where the editing was done and the headlines were written, was the most fantastic institution of the American newspaper scene. Like the city desk, it was a horseshoe, but it was far longer to accommodate a dozen or so copyreaders. In the slot sat Kenneth Davenport, the copydesk chief and the original mechanical man, lifting a story with his left hand, scanning it with a photographic eye as he moved it to his right hand, and then handing it to the first copyreader who wasn't busy.

Dav, as he was known, had a grim look acquired from dealing with new copyreaders. They blew in from every corner of the land, for the copyreaders of those days were nomads, and the *Her-Ex* was known far and wide as a haven for the wandering gentlemen who could write headlines. The only way to find out if they could was to try them.

The results were sometimes fantastic. Dav handed one new man an Associated Press story with the order to "cut it in two" —that is, edit it to half space. With one snip of his scissors the fellow carried out his instructions literally. "Which half do you want?" he asked the incredulous Dav.

First edition time was always a period of crisis at the *Her-*

Ex. There never seemed to be enough copyreaders to get the paper to press. At the height of one of these crises, a man walked in, looked respectfully at the assistant managing editor, Abe Geldhof, who was sitting in for Dav, and began: "I'm from . . ."

"Never mind telling me where you're from," interrupted Geldhof. "We don't think so much of the New Orleans *Picayune* and *The New York Times* here anyway, and that's where you guys always say you're from. You're hired. Sit down there and go to work."

He virtually threw the stranger into a chair on the rim of the copydesk and tossed him some stories to edit. Five minutes later he noticed that the stranger was staring bewildered at the copy and not writing any heads.

"Ever read any copy before?" asked Abe in a withering voice.

"No, sir," responded the stranger, happy to get anyone's attention in this madhouse into which fate had pushed him. "I'm from Walgreen's drugstore downstairs. I've got some aspirin for Mr. William Conway."

When one new copyreader wrote his first headline for Dav, it brought the comment, "That's the worst head I ever read in my life." The next evening he looked at another of the new copyreader's heads and snapped again, "That's the worst head I ever read in my life." "Worse than the one I wrote last night?" asked the hapless copyreader. "What was it?" demanded Dav. The newcomer told him. Dav thought a moment. "Yes," he then said reflectively, "worse than that."

Dav ran a no-nonsense desk. When he got a weather forecast from one copyreader and read, "Sunrise 6:42 A.M.," he shouted: "Never mind the 'A.M.' If it ever comes up in the P.M. it'll get three eight-column headlines."

A good managing editor was an eccentric one, and the eccentrics had a list of words and phrases which it was suicide for a writer to use. The editors below the banners remembered the words and phrases and kept them out, long after the man who banned them had departed.

In the long ago, one managing editor forbade the use of "cryptic" because he once saw it incorrectly used in the paper. Managing editors thereafter came and went, but the word was always kept out, because some of the editors weren't sure who had banned it originally, and others feared the editor who had banned it might see it from afar and have everyone fired if it appeared in the paper.

I spent thirteen years on the paper trying to get "cryptic" into print, but Dav, Geldhof, and their ilk spent the same years frustrating me. I tried to get it in as hopefully as Delos Avery tried for years to slip "And how are all your folks?" into a serious story. In another endeavor, Avery had spectacular success. He began a story about a neat and gentle old lady who had hanged herself with a reference to her reputation for neatness, and then he avoided telling what had happened in the closet where she was found until the last paragraph, which read: "And there they found Grandmother Wilson, hanging neat as a pin." They stopped the presses to take that one out, but they couldn't fire fun-loving Avery. He was one of the great feature writers of the day.

Geldhof's zeal for keeping banned words and deliberate sabotage like Avery's out of the paper was exceeded only by his enthusiasm for putting the most trivial railroad wrecks on Page One. That was because he had almost been fired for giving two paragraphs inside to a wreck that the *Tribune* had played on Page One with a 96-point headline. The wreck was in New York State and Robert M. Lee of the *Tribune* had happened to be aboard and had telegraphed a story.

The *Her-Ex* had definite ideas on the way the American family lived. It would have been treason to suggest to a *Her-Ex* editor that Mr. and Mrs. America didn't get up every morning with their stomachs so delicately adjusted that anything unpleasant they might read would spoil their breakfast completely. Bare feet were believed to be particularly revolting, and so feet could never be mentioned, because ours was a morning paper.

The word "socialite" was banned, not on the grounds of flippancy but because it was always getting into the paper as "socialist" and drawing threats of a libel suit from some capitalist or his wife.

Her-Ex Linotype men had a failing for making "rabbi" read "rabbit"; so "rabbi," while not banned, was looked upon as dynamite, never to be used when it was not absolutely necessary. Linotype men regarded it as one of the privileges of their trade to slip in embarrassing little errors which they hoped the proofreaders would fail to catch. Editors who were plagued by such antics might have enjoyed being with me when I visited a newspaper composing room for the first time in thirty-five years. The Linotype machines were there, but they were being operated by tapes, with the operators' chairs vacant.

Some of the banning was the stranger because so little was left to the imagination in *Her-Ex* stories otherwise. We might tell the most revolting details of a rape, yet the gentle reader must be kept in touching ignorance of the fact that it was a rape, for the *Her-Ex* was a family newspaper. All the editors said so. We must avoid the word and hide behind the term "attack." We were never permitted to whisper the word "abortion." Instead we used the more gruesome and infinitely more terrible "criminal operation." And husbands must not commit adultery; it was infidelity.

A whorehouse was neither that nor a house of prostitution. It was a "resort," which must have been confusing to readers who thought of resorts as seashore places or winter sports centers; its business was "vice." We could not write "prostitute," but we could publish a full-page picture in color of one if we merely called her a courtesan. We dared not say that a man had been castrated, although he might be mutilated, knifed, operated upon, or simply robbed of a gland, left or right.

Snakes and rats, like bare feet, were banned lest they offend breakfasters' weak stomachs. But in these modern days, morning papers delight in reporting that the body of the lady murder victim was "badly decomposed."

Hilding Johnson, hero of *The Front Page* (CHICAGO TRIBUNE)

Charles MacArthur and his wife, Helen Hayes (CHICAGO TRIBUNE)

Ben Hecht, co-author with Charles MacArthur of *The Front Page*

Harry Romanoff, who as Romy was the nation's number one police reporter (CHICAGO TODAY)

Marion Davies, actress and long-time friend of William Randolph Hearst
(CHICAGO TRIBUNE)

John (Dingbat) Oberta, lieutenant of Big
Tim Murphy and husband—before he too was
shot to death—of Big Tim's widow (CHICAGO
TRIBUNE)

Big Tim Murphy, pre-Capone king of Chicago gangland, killed by gangland
guns as he prepared to become an evangelist (CHICAGO TRIBUNE)

Aimee Semple McPherson, evangelist and professed enemy of Texas Guinan
(CHICAGO TRIBUNE)

CHAPTER 5

The *Her-Ex* was a paper truly beloved. We gave our readers what they wanted and they gave us credit for boons we never had dreamed of giving them, such as the Toonerville Trolley horse-betting service. The Toonerville Trolley was a somewhat incredible comic strip, in which the cartoonist, Fontaine Fox, underscored certain words, seemingly by a hit-and-miss system that had no relationship to emphasis or meaning.

The cartoons, of course, were drawn long in advance of the selection of the horses that would run in any specified race. Moreover, the cartoon, being a syndicated one, had the same words underscored in every city. Yet thousands of Chicagoans used to read in those underscored words the *Her-Ex*'s coded tips on races.

Policemen particularly relied on the Toonerville Trolley system despite their knowledge that most firemen would have none of it. Bettors had to guess for themselves, of course, just what it was that cartoonist Fox was trying to tell them, but the system worked as well as any that has ever been devised for beating the horse races. And the readers sang hosannas for the paper that even picked their horses for them.

Conscious of its adoration by its readers, the *Her-Ex* ever strove to give them more of what they wanted. We knew they liked stories about dogs, and so we gave them touching tales of dogs rescued from quarries. We gave them stories of millionaires, broken by the Depression, to whom policemen they had befriended made loans. We broke our readers' hearts and we made them laugh.

Harry Read, one of the great city editors for whom I worked, indeed had categories for stories:

"Tear their hearts out in two hundred words," he would tell me upon handing me some City News Bureau copy to rewrite. Or "Make me laugh." Or "Get indignant."

Back in 1922 an old lake captain known as the Christmas Tree Man went down with his ship and its load of Christmas trees in a fearsome storm on Lake Michigan on its run from Michigan to Chicago. When December came again, the *Her-Ex* published the story of his brave daughter, who was carrying on for the kiddies. She had sailed into Chicago harbor with a boatload of Christmas trees, as her father had done these many years before.

Next year it happened all over again. And the next. And the next. The story became an annual assignment. And the facts were always brought to me by Romy.

In December of 1937, on another paper by that time, I decided to dig up the annual story for myself. I called the captain's daughter to find out if she had sailed in yet with her shipload of Christmas trees.

"No," she told me. "We bring them in by truck. We've always used trucks or the train since Dad's boat went down."

"Why, what about those stories of you and your boat?" I asked as incredulously as could a newspaperman brought up in the philosophy that anything you wish to believe is true. "The *Her-Ex* prints them every year."

"Oh, you!" she exclaimed with an excited giggle. "Those

are just stories that Harry Romanoff dreamed up. He didn't want to disappoint the children."

A public that wore its heart on its sleeve was never disillusioned by the *Her-Ex*. When Vincenzo Celli returned to the United States as master of the ballet with the La Scala opera company, the paper dug up the fact that he had once been a Loop bootblack, and it wept a few tears over his Horatio Alger rise. Celli went back to Italy and returned to Chicago again. A concert dancer now of true renown, dividing his time between Chicago and New York, he wished to be known for his dancing alone. But he was doomed to frustration. The moment he announced a concert in Chicago he lost his status as a dancer and became, once more, the dark-eyed little Italian bootblack who made good.

The *Her-Ex* had a tremendous number of tipsters. Some wanted money for their information and some wanted publicity for themselves or revenge on their enemies. But by far the greatest number genuinely wished to help the paper. Some of those helpers almost put the paper out for us on New Year's Day.

There were doctors a-plenty who would hurry the stork up or delay him somewhat, in the hope of producing the last baby of the old year or the first of the new. They would telephone in immediately to report and counted that year lost when some sharpshooter sent his stork in ahead of theirs in a photo finish. The tipsters saw to it, too, that the *Her-Ex* got the first fire, first murder, first arrest, and first death.

I telephoned a Municipal Court judge one day to ask about a defendant who was appearing before him. It was a university professor who had gone bathing in the nude at Hyde Park beach, thinking he was concealed by trees. But a Peeping Tom old dowager in a skyscraper apartment on the beach had spied him with her binoculars and turned him in. The paper thought his arrest was very unfair indeed and wanted him freed. I explained the situation to the judge, for in those days judges would do anything for a friendly newspaper. But the judge got his signals crossed and presently called me triumphantly to report, "I sent the S.O.B. to the clink for a year."

Crooks who hated the guts of other crooks would call up to tell us who had committed a crime. Sometimes they would telephone just to get an enemy into trouble over something he hadn't done. Divorce lawyers, when they came to court, watched for Ray Quisno, greatest of court reporters. If they didn't see him, they would phone the facts of their trials to his office, just to make sure he wasn't scooped. They were accommodating souls.

An editor who chanced to read in a New York paper that a woman had sued for divorce on the grounds that her husband ran for President in off years, or raised hippos in their parlor, had only to pick up a telephone. There were half a dozen lawyers who would find a client to bring suit on the same grounds. The bar association used to send an investigator over occasionally to ask if what the association knew about slippery divorce lawyers was true. We always said, "Goodness, no."

The *Her-Ex* never missed an opportunity to play ball with its fans. Business executives who controlled hundred-million-dollar corporations were flattered pink to get from somebody on the paper a couple of free ducats to a six-day bicycle race or a dance marathon. It made them feel that they were rubbing elbows with the press, and at the exclusive Chicago Club they could casually mention getting tickets from "my friend Warren Brown," the paper's sports editor.

They joined phony press clubs in the hope of meeting working newspapermen, and seldom did they meet any of us without saying that they used to be newspapermen themselves. They were so insistent about press passes that our publisher, Homer Guck, eventually took our passes to the race tracks away from us and doled them out to advertisers on the theory that we had no business with them anyway unless we were actually covering the races.

Even the *Her-Ex* morgue (in these effete days the morgue has become the library) helped, in a purely accidental way, to cement the paper's friendship with the readers. Alarmed by the disappearance of books and clippings from the morgue, some innocents there had dreamed up the idea of stamping everything that could be lifted STOLEN FROM THE HERALD & EXAMINER MORGUE. Such items became collectors' prizes overnight, and half of Chicago got busy figuring out pretexts to visit the morgue and steal something so stamped. The souvenirs gave them status and made them feel themselves part of the *Her-Ex* family.

In an innocently wistful way, the paper made its heroes and villains neurotic by publishing their stories. Once they had seen their names in print, they couldn't sleep for wondering if they would be there again when they got up in the morning. They didn't care whether it was for philanthropy, stealing from poor boxes, or wife beating. It was being in print that mattered.

A man might spend his life in conservative clothes, thriftily piling up five million dollars, raising half a dozen kids, and being a reasonably discreet husband, and then, wham! Just as he was thinking of making it fifty million, he'd get himself involved with a blonde and find himself on Page One. Conservatism? It was a word for old fogies. On the second day he'd be calling the sob sisters by their first names. On the third, when the story had been pushed back to Page Eleven, he'd pose turning handsprings if they asked him to for just one more picture. He'd discovered that his involvement had made him a hero to the women he knew, a lion to the men, and gained him a new regard from his wife.

I saw a respectable old family caught up in one of the most spectacular murders of the century adjust itself to the white light of publicity. Sensitive, refined, all of them shrank instinctively from the newspapers. But the young daughter, bitterest of them all in her condemnation of the press, was persuaded to write her own story to raise defense funds for her mother. Overnight she became a changed girl—a working newspaperwoman, glamorous, uninhibited. She never got a chance to write another story, but from that time on the newspaper folk she had scorned were her friends, entertained in her home, introduced in her circles with pride. Her mother, a physician, went to prison, accused of murdering a daughter-in-law.

The Gallivanting Great Aunt, the Granite Grandmother, the Helpful Hermit: If you wanted to discover what publicity had done for them, you had only to wander into a convention, any kind of a convention, for they attended every meeting they heard about. Let it be known that you were from the *Her-Ex* and up would pop the GGA to remind you that it was your paper that hung the title on her for piloting an airplane at ninety.

She was at the convention, she would confess, in the hope that they might need an extra speaker and would call upon her to tell how she flew her own plane to Kalamazoo—upside down, mind you—at the age of eighty-nine. The Granite Grandmother, who kept on denying that she had murdered her husband until the charges were dropped years ago, would confess it to all who would listen and, knowing the case could not be reopened, tell exactly how she administered the arsenic.

The Helpful Hermit? He'd have thrown away his battered stovepipe hat and bought a new one that cost him $34. His hair would be just as long, but waved at the ends. His high boots would be shined. He'd tell you his metamorphosis into a well-dressed extrovert wouldn't interfere with his charities.

A Spartan Mother never forgot. Years after she had sent a son away to prison because he was a louse, and won *Her-Ex* acclaim and her title, she would be calling up late at night to say she'd had her husband arrested today, the drunken bum—in the hope that she'd get a paragraph in the market section to remind her of the grand old days when she hit Page One.

More loyal even than those the paper had lionized were those it panned. They telephoned in every tip they thought might make news, proud of their knowledge that the place to call was the city desk. When a member of the family died, they were on the phone with the obit, and they always reminded the reporter, "I'm the girl your paper tagged 'Gorgeous Gertie' in that alienation of affections suit," or, "You'll remember me. You called me 'Precious Paul, the gigolo.'"

Previous thrills from seeing their names in the paper, I have no doubt, accounted for the many women who reported that they had been raped when they hadn't. One of the few who objected to being in the paper was a gangland sweetheart we had titled the Kiss of Death because her lovers were forever getting killed. She complained that it made new suitors nervous and this interfered with her love life.

Another objector was Tough Tony Capezio. He didn't mind being called a gangland assassin, a bomber, or a bootlegging boss. It was the "Tough" that devastated him.

"I got kids in school," he would protest tearfully. "They get razzed by the other kids about that Tough Tony. Call me anything you want. But please, leave the Tough out."

A man who was grateful for past favors (we sometimes revised the Tough Tony in later editions and alluded to him as plain Tony), he always ended his telephone calls with the assurance that he would bump off anyone we wanted erased, "and it won't cost you a dime."

Most distinguished of the *Her-Ex* helpers were the society women and businessmen on our symposium list. They numbered more than four hundred and were the social, financial, civic, and intellectual leaders of the community, most of them with a love of seeing their names in print.

Did Wilbur Glenn Voliva decide the world wasn't flat after all, or recant his teaching that eating oysters was a sin because they didn't have feathers? The staff dropped its work and got on the telephone to ask everyone on the symposium list for comment on the religious fanatic's latest pronouncement. If Irene Castle McLaughlin demanded swift punishment for medical researchers who practiced vivisection on dogs, we asked the members of the city elite what they thought.

We didn't spare the Swifts, the Armours, the Meekers, the Fields, the Higginbothams. They might not be interested in who killed Billy McSwiggin, were Sally Rand's fans too revealing, should Rogers Hornsby be fired, was Samuel Insull's utilities empire crumbling, was Queen Marie of Rumania a snob, was Hinky Dink Kenna a menace to the community, should Mayor Big Bill Thompson be impeached for his crack about punching King George in the nose, was Marion Davies the greatest actress of the century? But, interested or not, they came up with comments, which the paper published the following day.

CHAPTER 6

Because reporters with ideas were always welcome at the *Her-Ex*, no matter how fantastic their ideas might be, Harold Cross was held in high esteem. He had a lively imagination and a notebook when he came. With a little encouragement he threw away the notebook. Ordered one day to produce a story if he had to manufacture it, news was so dull, Cross took literally the instructions he had received from city editor Duffy Cornell (Duffy in the MacArthur-Hecht play *The Front Page*). He departed and telephoned back with a whimsical tale of a Chinese laundryman who had vanished, leaving half of fashionable Lake Forest's business giants with no clean shirts.

Messrs. Cross and Cornell both narrowly escaped losing their jobs the next day. The address Cross had given for the laundry turned out to be that of *Her-Ex* publisher Babe Meigs, the former University of Chicago football star.

It was the same Harold Cross who conceived the story of Peg Leg Nell. She was a horse, a simple horse, as sound of body as of mind, who worked faithfully at her task of drawing a junkman's wagon around suburban Hammond and never dreamed of fame and fortune. But Cross met her and, without breathing his intentions into her unsuspecting ear, decided to glorify her in the *Her-Ex*.

As Cross got the story, by going into a Cross trance, Peg Leg Nell—until that moment known as Old Mike—was going down the street at noon on three of her own legs and a wooden one fashioned for her by an ingenious artisan. As fate or Mr. Cross would have it, a gasoline truck overturned, spilling its inflammable load upon the pavement. Peg Leg Nell, or Old Mike if you will, kicked a spark. It ignited the gasoline which, not to be outdone, ignited Peg Leg Nell's peg leg, burning it off. Delos Avery gave the Cross facts the Avery treatment.

The next day Peg Leg Nell's owner came in, weeping. He said he had been laughed out of the suburb that he had served as junkman for lo these many years, and now he had no way of earning a living in his declining days. He wanted damages. Thoughtfully, Avery went back to his caterpillar tank.

In those days famed G-man Melvin Purvis was tracking down outlaw John Dillinger. Reporter Joe Hanson was currently the fair-haired boy of the reportorial staff, because he had modestly confided to the city editor that, in addition to being a phenomenal reporter, he had gone to school with Purvis.

Hanson, who referred to Purvis fondly as Mel, was obviously the man to shadow the elusive sleuth. Since there was nobody like an old schoolmate to tip you off as to when he was going to catch or rub out bad man Dillinger, he got the assignment and headed for Purvis's office.

Hanson was demanding the news of the Dillinger search in the lobby of Purvis's office when Dave Mann, a top *Her-Ex* photographer, strolled in. The ace reporter was taking no back talk from Uncle Sam. Said he to the slight young man who was patiently explaining that there would be no bulletins that day:

"Do I have to go over your head to my old school chum, Mel?"

The photog tapped Hanson on the shoulder. "That," Mann said, "is Mr. Purvis you're talking to."

Dillinger, the most notorious bank robber of the Thirties, was subsequently shot to death by Purvis and his agents as the outlaw emerged from a Chicago movie theater. The bank robber had been betrayed by his latest sweetie, known as The Lady in Red.

Hilding Johnson, whom MacArthur and Hecht immortalized with the *Her-Ex* in *The Front Page,* talked with me by telephone for years. But, since he never came into the office (he had his pay mailed to him at his beat in the Criminal Courts building), I never saw him until he lay dead in his casket.

And I can assure you that he didn't look the way he sounded. Telephone reporters never do. If they have full, lusty voices, they're timid little men, and if they call you Mister in a childish treble, they look like gorillas. You can't trust them. Well, Hilding Johnson (Hildy, the playwrights called him) hated detail as fiercely as he loved the unusual.

He never missed a fact on an important story. He scooped the town by piecing together a murder jury's torn ballots and then marking more ballot forms—wrong—for the other reporters to find in shreds on the floor of the jury room. While rival papers were printing the wrong verdict, with the explanation that it was a scoop in print before the verdict was even read in court, Hilding's paper was publishing the right one. But this brooding giant couldn't be persuaded to waste his talent and energy on a minor story. After he had broken his leg, it became increasingly difficult for rewrite men to snare information from him.

Rewrite man Arthur Turney recorded verbatim Hilding's report on one story, as Hilding telephoned it in:

"H'lo, Art. This is Hilding Johnson, out West here in this goddamned Criminal Courts building, halfway to I.O.U. Now, you understand this is all horseshit, Art. It's about a guy named Rogers. You can get his first name out of the clippings. Well, he's up in court again today.

59

"Wait a minute, Art, 'til I chase these lousy bastards out of the press room. Get out of here, you bastards. H'lo, Art. Just chasing some bastards out so I can hear. Of course you realize, Art, this story's all horseshit. You'll have to look up the charge in the morning paper. Since I broke my left leg I can't get around to clean up these stories like I used to, Art. You can get everything out of the afternoon papers. I've lost my notes. Anyway, Art, it's all horseshit."

Johnson was not inclined to pussyfoot. When an assistant state's attorney named William McSwiggin was murdered—the victim, papers charged, of an alliance between the underworld and politicians—Johnson was assigned to annoy a certain public official by going daily to his office with the query "Who killed Billy McSwiggin and why?" He always telephoned his report on the hapless official's own phone. "City desk?" he would inquire. "Hilding Johnson speaking. I'm out here in the office of John P. for Prick Anderson to ask him who killed Billy McSwiggin and why. The bastard says he doesn't know."

A cub reporter was told one morning to cover a children's party on board Commander Eugene McDonald's yacht, *Mizpah*. Because the Zenith tycoon was a friend of all the editors, the day city editor told the reporter: "Take good care of Gene McDonald. He's one of our sacred cows."

Back from the party, the tyro began his story: "Commander Eugene McDonald, a sacred cow . . ."

One morning at one of the wire services it was reported that the Pullman Company was going to have to stop building stainless steel cars because it couldn't get steel. I telephoned Pete Vroom, the crusty old press agent for Pullman, and asked him about it. I said I hoped I wasn't troubling him, calling him so late at night.

"Oh, no, Shon," he said, "I jhust shtay up at nights waiting for calls from zhe Herland and Exshaiminger. Wait a minute and I'll ghive you a shtatement."

Presently he was on the phone again. "I hope you could understand me," he said quite clearly. "You woke me up and I couldn't find my goddamn teeth. Now here's the statement about our inability to get material for the cars. It won't bother us. Material is immaterial."

Sent to interview a public official accused of stealing a few hundred thousand dollars, Earl Mullen, commonly called Moon because of the cartoon strip, had the door slammed in his face by a maid who said in flawless diction, "I am sorry, but I do not speak one word of English."

Ham Bailey was so enchanted by his work on our paper that he moved into a hotel across the street, to be closer when he was needed. The editors thereafter called him at any time they might find him useful and rewarded him handsomely for his enthusiasm with late assignments and no overtime.

Ham was the confidential aide of the night city editor, who was trying to fall off the water wagon in the face of discouraging efforts by the management to keep him on. Chin up, despite terrific odds, the editor was making a winning fight when he ran out of liquor.

The managing editor, knowing this to be the night, had assigned Pat Daugherty, the woman rewrite man, to sit all night beside the city desk, a sentry who must let no liquor pass through the line to the man who was determined to fall off.

The editor crooked a stealthy finger at Ham.

"Go across the street to the speakeasy," he commanded, "and get me a pint of gin."

Pat followed Ham out into the hall.

"Don't bring that guy any gin," she said. "Managing editor's orders. If you do, you're fired."

"And if I don't, I'm fired," Ham replied philosophically. "It's just a question of whether I'm fired by my boss or the managing editor. My boss is the man who sits in the city desk slot. If the managing editor doesn't want me to follow my boss's orders, he ought to put somebody else there."

In five minutes, Ham was back. Pat watched him pass the bottle to the city editor, who promptly set about getting so fried that he began a spree that continued for a month.

Next morning Ham was fired for obeying the newspaperman's first rule: take your orders from the man in the slot.

He ended his *Her-Ex* career in a blaze of glory, running from telephone booth to telephone booth in the Loop, turning in fire and burglar alarms. When the police finally caught up with him in his room he asked for a moment to get his coat, ducked out the window, and ran away to join the navy.

The strangest of all the *Her-Ex* personages came in the later years, an affable young man who covered the Board of Trade. One morning he came in bubbling; he had a tip on wheat futures. He was going to make a killing. Over his protests, the blasé staff persuaded him to let them in. Everyone from the managing editor to the copyboys pressed money into his hand to plunge for them on his tip. One copyboy, indeed, was so late getting back from the bank with his savings that he had to chase the market wizard down the street with his money.

The market wizard was never seen again.

Jean Ladour will do for the name of the bright-eyed little continental who got a job on the *Her-Ex* in the mysterious way that completely unequipped gentlemen sometimes did. He had degrees from several foreign universities and a journalism degree from Columbia. His English was that clipped, flawless kind that foreigners so often acquire, but he could not understand our ways, our news, or our slang. He was forever coming out with some barrelhouse phrase while interviewing one of the grand old ladies of the W.C.T.U. or the D.A.R., who would complain to the management. Investigation invariably disclosed that he had learned the offending language from some joyous little sob sister who delighted in imparting off-color language to him with the assurance that it meant something quite complimentary.

But he was so happy and so polite that no one had the heart to let him starve to death. And so, when it became apparent that he would never become a reporter, the editors, unaware that he was writing a book on the infantilism of Americans who cleaned up forty thousand dollars a year editing newspapers, assigned him to carrying plates for photographers and other menial tasks.

The Catholic Eucharistic Congress changed all that. The obscure plate carrier was suddenly transformed into a linguist who could chat with the princes of the church from all over the world in their own languages. He scooped the world on news while awaiting instructions from a $35-a-week photographer. For the duration of the Congress, he was the paper's ace newsgetter. The amazing reversal of his fortunes and his contact with the world religious leaders did strange things to Jean, who called himself Johnnie. When the editors noticed, they sent him to a hospital.

There he would solemnly summon the nurses, and admonish them, "I am God. Do as I say." On alternate days he would call them in to tell them, somewhat sheepishly, "I'm not God. I just told you that. I'm only Johnnie Ladour of the *Herald & Examiner.*"

Crime reporter Maurice Roddy was genuinely the pal of a great many big-time gangsters, for a crime reporter had to hobnob with the underworld figures to find out what they were doing. When the government was on the trail of Murray-the-Camel Humphreys, who knew he'd eventually have to surrender and explain why he hadn't paid his income tax, he went dodging around the city for days, trying in vain to persuade Roddy to take him in, surrender him, and claim credit for the capture of Public Enemy Number 1.

It was Roddy who named the Walking Bomb after that denizen of the underworld told him, "I've laid so many sticks [bombs are pineapples to the public only] that I can't count 'em, any more than you can count the number of cigarettes you've smoked in your life." Roddy gave him that appellation when the police finally caught up with the Walking Bomb and treated him very gently when he told them, "Be careful. I've got enough soup on me to blow up the Loop"—which was the truth.

There was nothing underhanded about the Walking Bomb. Before he bombed you, he'd send you a message: "Christmas is coming." If it weren't the Christmas season, and you were a Chicagoan, you'd know that something odd was going to happen to you. Wasn't that fair?

It was Roddy who thought of planting Spike O'Donnell, the handsomest and most urbane of Chicago's gangsters, on the roof of the city hall when a distinguished British writer came to town to learn about gangland. Since Spike had just been invited to England to play Robin Hood in a British movie, the Englishman was especially anxious to see him in his native habitat.

Spike was meditatively looking over the city, like a monarch over his domain, when the Englishman caught sight of him. Gravely Spike shook hands, chatted a moment about the problems of ruling with a gun a city of three and one-half million population. Then, while Roddy got the visitor away, Spike ran like hell lest the police hear about Roddy's latest gag and toss Spike into the bucket on general principles.

Roddy was there the night they found out about Herman the Great. Not the magician; he spelled it differently. The newsboy.

Herman the Great knew Chicago's gangsters by their first names, and Chicago's first-nighters too, for he sold them papers along the Loop Rialto at night. Yesterday's papers. They didn't cost anything, and Herman the Great knew his customers didn't want to read them anyway. They merely wanted to hand Herman the Great a dime, because it was customary and he needed the money.

He was a sort of amiable barfly, who got fat on the free

meals the kindly restaurateurs gave him at their back doors, but who never seemed to spend any of the money the night-lifers gave him for new clothes. At sixteen, he was still wearing the same ragged overcoat he had worn at twelve, with the same rope tied around it for buttons. The oversize garment fit better, though, for he was growing into it.

A fattish boy in ragged clothes was killed by an automobile on the Rialto one afternoon. He was unidentified until William Botham, the steak house man, looked upon him and said he was Herman the Great. No one knew his real name. Next day his mother came down to find out why Herman the Great hadn't been home. They told her about the accident, and she told them some rather pathetic things about Herman the Great. He was the only support of the traditional family of nine children, in the days before welfare had been established. There really were nine. That was why he never bought any clothes for himself. He would have carried the free meals home if he hadn't been afraid the people who gave them to him wouldn't understand. Although he had been a Loop landmark for four years, he never had been downtown in the daytime until the day he was killed, for he had to sleep most of the day. He hadn't been accustomed to the Loop in daytime, his mother conjectured, and the Rialto looked strange to him without the blazing lights, so strange that he became confused when he saw the onrushing automobile and forgot to step out of the way.

CHAPTER 7

I had come from the Indiana town of Frankfort (population then 11,885) which boasted three daily papers, the *Times,* the *News,* and the *Crescent,* in those forgotten days when even little cities had more than one newspaper and the big ones half a dozen to a dozen. I worked briefly on all three of the Hoosier dailies and then went on to Chicago to fall in love with a profession that was to make me a correspondent in Washington and in Moscow.

Three times I asked politely for an interview with the city editor of the Chicago *Herald & Examiner.* Twice I tried to slip past the burly doorman whose wooden arm came off so easily to make a club. But one day I saw a reporter in the hall vanish before me through a side door—the same side door, I later learned, that Charlie MacArthur used to avoid passing the desk of his first wife, Carol Frink, the movie critic, when he came in on his trips between Hollywood and New York, after he had become a playwright, to kiss the bald head of paunchy, garlicky Harry Romanoff.

I followed the reporter in. A moment later I found myself in the great city room. It was old even then, and cluttered with the wreckage of the dozen or more newspapers that were its ancestors. The physical part of the strange institution known as the city desk must have begun life as a place for some gloomy editor of Paper Number 1 to work alone. Each time a helper was added to his retinue it must have been enlarged by the carpenter until it had become an enormous, sprawling horseshoe, in imminent danger of falling apart. Over it ran a maze of old gas pipes from the gaslight days, from which electric lights were now strung.

Under the somewhat cockeyed bower they formed, the city editor stacked each edition of the afternoon papers, the packages he meant to take home to his wife, and anything else that seemed to be in his way. He sat in the slot, the inside of the horseshoe, scowling out at assistants who sat on the rim, at the rewrite men whose desks faced him, and at the reporters whose desks were ranged row after row behind the rewrite men.

The great copydesk, where the editing was done, was a horseshoe too. Like the city desk, it had been patched and expanded for decades; yet it seemed somehow to have a better chance of holding together throughout the day.

Eddie Hafferkamp took me in tow. He was the man who sat opposite the city editor, answering telephone calls and making out the assignments for reporters. This Eddie did in an informal but effective way. Modern papers maintain an assignment book, and reporters, when they come to work, read it to learn their tasks for the day. Eddie merely kept a cabinet, with drawers for the current and succeeding month. Into the proper drawers he dropped clippings and memos. Each day he opened the proper drawer and made his assignments. Although I didn't know it at the time, I was later to realize that Eddie was a jewel. With deft assurance, he solved the domestic problems of the city editor. When an editor or a reporter went on a binge, Eddie made it right with the angry wife.

He waved away my credentials, my letter of recommendation from the mayor of my hometown, and my Hoosier newspaper clippings, for life was easy in the golden days of the early Twenties, when editors chartered special trains to cover out-of-town stories. Eddie didn't really care about those things, for he knew I was being hired only because the staff was being built up against the inevitable time when orders for a staff cut, the dreaded shake-up, would come from Mr. Hearst, whom every one of us knew as The Chief. Then I and other supernumeraries could be fired without endangering the nucleus of the staff, and the paper could claim credit for drastic economies. Any smart Hearst editor hired people he didn't need when times were good. And there happened to be enough money left in the budget for me.

The trial of Nathan Leopold and Richard Loeb for the murder of little Bobby Franks was then in progress. I had seen the crowds trying to get in from the elevated train when I went job-hunting at the *Her-Ex*. And I had visions, when I telephoned next morning, of hearing Eddie say the paper was short staffed at the trial and would I go down. Instead, he told me to interview President Ernest De Witt Burton of the University of Chicago upon his return from Europe.

At eleven that night, I began my second shift of the day, for your body belonged to the *Her-Ex* in the days before the wages and hours laws. My night's work was to stop all taxicabs arriving at the women's dormitories in the hope of finding and interviewing Frank A. Vanderlip's daughter, Charlotte, when she arrived from New York to matriculate.

I was still stopping them in vain at breakfast time, for the *Her-Ex* strategy was to keep you on the doorstep until you got what it wanted or else died from old age. Many a cabdriver whose door I opened raced on in terror because the timid souls inside the cab thought I was a holdup man. Charlotte had arrived a day early, unbeknownst to us.

I didn't make myself exactly popular at the university. I crashed a private meeting of faculty members with Queen Marie of Rumania. I barged in on Dr. Albert A. Michelson, famed for measuring the speed of light. In high dudgeon, he drove me from his office—when I asked him how he had done it—and vowed to teach me a lesson in manners. At his behest, I went to the nearest telephone, asked for an interview, and was invited to return immediately. He seemed inclined to let the matter drop, but I heard about it from my office. Long years afterward, I understood. His brother was the public relations man Charles Michelson, later to be the famed public relations director for the National Democratic Committee, and he didn't want reporters coming in to see his brother without an appointment.

I brought in photographers to take pictures of coeds, in brazen defiance of a ruling by Henry Justin Smith that they couldn't be photographed on campus without his personal permission, which was difficult to get. Henry had recently retired as managing editor of the Chicago *Daily News* to direct the university's public relations, and he had strict ideas. When a university official got himself shot in Mandel Tower, he explained that he was protecting the honor of a girl. I started to dig and got the word to lay off. I did, although the city editor, Jack Malloy, told me I was giving up too easily.

My worst offense was my discovery that a group of science professors had invited a British clairvoyant by the improbable name of Mazie to address them on campus. It was a hush-hush affair, to be held behind closed doors at midnight. I learned about it, and we published the story. Such activities ended my campus reporting days.

I asked to be moved into the city room, and the editors okayed it. My job was to take memos by telephone from reporters at police stations or at the scenes of crimes. That's how I got into the big time.

Hearst's greatest columnist, Arthur Brisbane, spent most of his time in New York, or at Mr. Hearst's San Simeon ranch, writing his Page One column, "Today." It was a lively, fundamentalist column that rarely failed to mention man's superiority over the ape, or the fortunes to be made in real estate that Brisbane was reputed to own.

I never saw him except once in my life, but that was a momentous occasion. He had stopped off in Chicago on his way to San Simeon and had come in to inspect the *Her-Ex*. The rewrite men, who wove the stories from the facts telephoned in by the reporters, were the elite of the newspaper world in those days.

They sat at tiers of typewriters facing the city desk, and, like kings in their crowns, they worked with their hats on. They were grizzled veterans, all of them earning the unbelievable salary in those days of $150 a week or more. I worked for $40 a week.

Brisbane and news editor William Conlon came slowly past, staring at the rewrite men and then at me. They came back twice to watch me, and then halted.

"Young man," Brisbane told me, "this paper has the greatest rewrite staff in the United States. We even have a woman rewrite man. [Her name was Patricia Daugherty, and she was the greatest, a brunette beauty who could interview Al Capone any time she wanted to.] But we don't have a rewriter who types by the touch system. You do. From now on you are a rewrite man."

I put on my hat and joined the royalty.

I did my homework: studied the style of Delos Avery, who wrote the funniest features I have ever read, and Arthur Turney, the master of the action story; and finally my chance came.

Big Tim Murphy, king of Chicago's gangland in the pre-Capone days, was assassinated. He was in his bungalow on Chicago's North Side, listening by radio to the Republican convention in Kansas City that first nominated Herbert Hoover for President, when the doorbell rang. Wise in the ways of gangland, Big Tim slipped out a side door to investigate. Wise in the ways of Big Tim, the assassins mowed him down with machine guns from a car in the street.

I drew the assignment to write the story. The *Herald & Examiner* at that time had six editions, which came out from 6 P.M. to 7 A.M. I took the information from Romy and from a dozen reporters who were on the scene. And I literally wrote all night: the original bulletin, the original story, additions of new facts, Big Tim's history, and complete new stories for each edition.

Big Tim came to life again, the six-foot-four giant who directed the Dearborn station mail robbery; the politician in a gates-ajar collar and a claw-hammer coat who got himself elected to the Illinois House of Representatives with the slogan "Vote for Big Tim Murphy—He's a Cousin of Mine"; the cop-hating gangster who complained that the police would pick him up for spitting on the sidewalk; the self-effacing Big Tim who told the voters he never got to college but went to "de swimmin' school," though he insisted the band play "On Wisconsin" at his rallies; the man who loved opera and hobnobbed at the opera house with the Samuel Insull set; the man who tried to become an evangelist but said he was frustrated by the police, who wouldn't stop slapping him in jail.

When the last word had been written, I sat back and waited for Jack Malloy to approach me with the newspaperman's accolade, "Good story!"

He approached all right, and his words are still etched on my memory, more than four decades later. Said Malloy:

"My God! Wouldn't it be my luck to have the story of the year breaking and you the only rewrite man I had free!"

Lesser men might have been discouraged by the rebuff of my story of Big Tim. But I remembered the old story that Alfred Tennyson glorified King Arthur's knights of the round table after failing as a writer for some British weekly. So I set out to tell Big Tim's story, and the stories of other gangsters, in verse:

BIG TIM

Big Tim the bluff, Big Tim the boisterous,
Big Tim, the king of all Chicago's gangs,
Took off his hat. A bronze-haired rewrite girl

71

Glanced up, shook hands, and bade the giant sit.
"You need an alibi," she said. "You come to me
That you in court one day may tell the judge:
'Here's Pat. I chewed the fat with her that hour
When Ike the Torch was bumped. My tommy gun
Went all unused. She nods, so spring me, Judge.'
You sit and chat with me, Big Tim, but well
I know that dismal Hegewisch or Oak Park
Resounds the while your guns rub someone out."

The gangster smiled. "I'd be a dope, uts-nay,
A wackie-dack, to try to bunco you,
Friend Pat, the sharpest girl the paper's got.
No. Harmless as a lamb—that's me today.
Ah, Pat, I come to see your smile once more,
And hear the dirt on Con Man Yellow Kid.
He peddles klucks the city hall no more,
I'm told, but lets them bet him he can't spin
The Hotel Sherman 'round, its back to front
By pulling levers, bingo!"
                                    So they spoke
Of Yellow Kid, and gangland's wars, but ere
Their words had ceased the switchboard lights
Flashed red upon the city desk; the wires
Brought news. "Two gangsters shot!" reporters shout.
"The cops accuse Big Tim. Dragnets are out.
'Lock up Big Tim,' the captains tell their men.
'We've got the goods on him this time, for all
Can see: his rivals grew too strong. Big Tim
Decreed their death.' "
                                    Big Tim arose. "And now,"
To Pat, "I'd better duck. I'm warm—nay—hot.
Remember when you write, Big Tim was here
From two o three to three on nine. The job,
You'll find, was sharp at three o one. Good luck."

"Two gangsters slain," the judge proclaimed in court
Next day. "Big Tim, you stand suspect. Your plea?"
"Me mouthpiece talks." Big Tim displayed his chain
of gold, his trousers striped, his coat of black,
His collar gates ajar, his sparkling gem
Beneath. His raiment shamed his counsellor's,
The bailiff's e'en.
                            The lawyer spoke. "A writ,
Or make the coppers book him, Judge. You'll find
They've nothing on him, never have. Big Tim
They toss into the klink for fun. They lock
Him up for packing concealed ideas.
Your honor, we can bring to court today
A *Her-Ex* girl, one Pat, to testify
Big Tim was at her desk from two o three
To three on nine. All know these mugs were bumped
Eight miles away at three o one.
This Pat speaks only truth. Shall we call her, or will
The prosecution yield?"
                            "Okay! Okay."
The state's attorney yielded thus his case,
In courtly tongue. "But watch your step, Big Tim,
We'll pick you up for spitting on the walk,
Or slap you in the jug for vagrancy."
"Who, me—a vag? Bunco!" The giant beamed.
"And me with seven grand here in me kick.
Big Tim, the man the voters of this state
Chose representative on this here plank:
Vote Twice for Swell Big Tim—My Cousin, Boys.
You're nutty as a fruit cake, Toots.
You'll be—forgive my language, Judge—
A-cutting paper dolls and building things
With blocks, when I'm your senator. I'm off
To visit Santa Claus. Send me my mail
In care the reindeer, Twelve O Four North Pole,

Or try the Mayflower, Washington, D.C.,
Where me and Dingbat sips our demi-tasse."

His gray fedora waved Big Tim aloft
In tribute to the black-robed man of law,
Then joined his men, who tarried in the hall,
Dingbat, Three-Fingered Joe, the faithful Genk.
"A matchless wit." His Honor glowed. "A gem,
Albeit somewhat rough. A stout man at
The polls. May he recall me pleasantly
Come next election time. Court stands adjourned."

Down blazed the sun. The horse of iron took rest,
And men in workers' garb played ball the while
The train puffed into Dearborn station grim.
Anon they put their ball away, roused up,
Drew guns, and on the mail car sprang with shouts.
They stripped it of its gold; enough was there
To ransom kings. The guards, bewildered, watched,
Then gave alarm. But whooping through the shed,
The robbers fled in owlish glee.
                              No maid
With tresses bronze there was in court
That day Big Tim looked twelve men in the face,
A jury of his peers; no maid to say
Big Tim had sat beside her as she wrote,
The while the men who played at ball had robbed
The mail. Some said Big Tim, none else, was chief
Of all the robber gang.
                           "Big Tim, who taught
The underworld to use the tommy gun."
The prosecutor glowered upon the court.
"And gave to Illinois the one-way ride."

"The rap is bum!" Big Tim arose, and then
Sank back upon his haunch. "No cop court this,"

His lawyer warned. "Keep tightly closed your trap."
"I know, I know." The giant breathed a sigh.
"The old man with the whiskers follows me—
The G. No educated cookie I—
Mine was de swimmin' school, but still I know
Dey'll put me under glass. Psychology!
And umpteen calendars dey'll tear to bits,
The Democrats dey'll have in power before
Dey let me on a choo-choo bound for home."

Long time the jurors weighed his fate. "Big Tim?
Who else could have contrived the game of ball?
He's guilty." Yet the twelve no haste would brook
In meting justice out. Chicago knew
Big Tim, the widow's son, to mother kind.
Why, Curci, Garden, Insull might he greet
By given name. The Armours and the Swifts
Big Tim might slap upon the back, or hail
With lusty voice on opening nights perchance
The mayor e'en. A killer? Yes, no doubt.
But merit in his killings few denied.
The town were better for them. Rock the Rat
And Trouble Tribble, Dottie Dan. Was none
Who might gainsay Big Tim had chosen well.
A robber? True. But infinitely more—
A Robin Hood, who took from those who had
To share with those who lacked. A racketeer?
Nay—labor chief, the workers' friend. His men
All struck when striking he decreed. Were some
Would say employers bought his soul with gold,
And water carried he fore'er on both
His shoulders broad. A million had he made
And lost. His motto yet for all his men:
A Better Deal. State representative
He'd been, the great song of America
Had pledged to pen; a lulu, nothing less.

'Gainst all his civic deed he weighed the charge.
"Three hundred fifty grand," they said. "Too much.
The balance seems to lie with crime. His guilt
Is clear. To Leavenworth Big Tim must go."

The calendars were torn. Big Tim was free.
Bands played for his return. The town once more
Was gay. Big Tim was back, and all was well.
The patient copy desks gave thanks. *Big Tim*
Was short, would fit in e'en the ninety-six
point line. Full inches less than Scarface Al
Capone, Machine Gun Jack McGurn, and all
The Clan Aiello. Ammunition Ed
And Diamond Lou Alterie ne'er should plague
Their deadline time again.
                              Big Tim them all
Would overshadow day and night and crowd
From tight Page One to Seventeen. And they
Might lucky be to find themselves upon
The page obituary in the Five
Star Final run. Reporters, too, rejoiced.
Big Tim, they knew, made news by columns long,
Not printer's sticks. His song a lulu was,
Composed in prison. Now he flew to grow
The grapefruit rich, in Texas sands; returned
In chaps and Western hat, ten-gallon size.
"Evangelist!" cried he. "Religion's now
Me racket. Texas ranger parson, late
Of jail. I'll wow 'em if the cops will let
Me stay outside the klink. But first I'll bring
A better deal, a pip, to all the maids
And butlers of Chicago's Gold Coast fair.
A union—that's their need. I'll break their legs
Unless they let me give them their reward,
The monkeys. Dues they'll pay. And I can use
A little lettuce."

The G.O.P. in staid convention sat.
The radio brought news that K.C. choice
Might Hoover be for President. Big Tim
Approved. And then the front door bell was heard.
"The mobs," Big Tim recalled, "don't wish me well.
They'd plug me if they could." The gangster wise
In gangland's ways, the front door scorned, stealt out
The side upon the lawn. Too late he saw
The car. The guns of gangland mowed him down.

The copy desks gave thanks. *Big Tim* was short;
Would fit, in e'en the ninety-six point line.

TWENTY-ONE

The Bear still sat with back to wall. Twelve years
As gangland chief and yet he sat, his gaze
Upon the door through which one day would come
The men, tight-lipped, to take him to his death.
Four guards, tight-lipped as those he feared, all knew
Stood ever in the hall; and yet he watched,
For guards he trusted not, nor any man.
The Bear relied upon himself, had seen
The guns of gangland claim the chiefs who placed
Their trust in others. Now the door his son
Flung open, ran to sit upon his knee and pat
The pistol blue The Bear had drawn in haste,
Had taken from its drawer when he heard steps.

"All A's!" The lad read off the grades with pride.
"Big stuff!" The gangster smiled. "You stick to books.
You'll show these monkeys yet your Pop's okay.
Here's half a C. Tell Mom you need a suit.
You'll soon be twelve. You ought to wear long pants."

The door, ajar, swung wide once more. The men,
Tight-lipped, had come. "Your gat," said one, "just drop

It on the floor. No need to buzz for your
Gorillas. One's rubbed out. The rest have ducked—
For ice cream cones." The Bear knew well his time
Had come. "The kid," said he. "I'll need some time
To send him home." The killers said, "No gags.
We go right now, or let you have it here."
From out his chair they dragged The Bear in haste.
"Get going now!" The chief assassin grim
Brooked no delay. The boy their mission knew.
"You bump my father, Rats," he said, "and I
Will kill you when I'm grown a man." They laughed.
The boy they pushed aside; his sire they took
Upon a one-way ride.

                    The candles burned
One day upon a cake, full twenty-one. Young Rik
Took aim. The flames went out, no leaden slug
That missed its mark. "Your pardon, friends." He waved
A gay salute. The barroom louts crawled out
From 'neath the tables they had used as shields.
"I celebrate a big event. My birthday. You
Must share my cake before I go to claim
An old revenge, my father's office too,
And pop a few gorillas, nothing more.
There's cake for all, and lead for some I know."

Three gangsters died that night. A slender youth
Met Lilac Joe and Dan the Dip upon the street.
"Remember me?" The youth drew off his hat and showed
The gun within. "Just put 'em up. And have
A look at me. The Bear was my old man.
And you're the mugs who bumped him. Boys, the time
Has come for you to pay. I'm twenty-one.
You may recall I told you I'd grow up."
The pistol roared, the papers said, and he
Strode blithely off.

Machine Gun Mack sat back
To wall, where once The Bear had sat. He ruled
The gang that once had held The Bear its lord,
When he sat back to wall and face to door. "My men,"
The gang chief mused, "Wait in the hall, and yet
I'm jittery and think too much of days
Long past, see shades."

"No shades, I'm real." The youth
Had entered all unseen. "Put down the gun.
And save your breath. Your guards are all tied up.
I told you once I'd get you, rub you out.
You killed The Bear and now you're on the spot."
The prosecutors tried a month to reason why
Three gangsters died that night, for gangland wars,
They knew, had long been ended by a truce.
Machine Gun Mack's lieutenants gave no clue
But took their orders thenceforth from a youth
Who ever sat with back to wall—a youth
They paid respect, and feared, and called The Cub.

SAMOOTS

Now came a day of black misfortune to Samoots.
His Stradivarius, which long had charmed
The West Side's hosts, was crushed beneath a truck,
A truck of giant's size that trundled beer
For Yukon's gang. A sadder mien Smoots
Had seldom worn than on that morn when all
His songs were stilled. His anger rose. "May you
And all your mob wind up in Hell!" His fist
He shook at Yukon's driver. "X shall mark
The spot my violin you crushed, my soul as well.
I'll see your gang rubbed out, your bones encased
In fresh concrete, and dropped in vengeance meet
Into the mire o'er which unceasing flows

The Sanitary District's foul canal.
And you shall rot 'midst bones of men
Long gone on rides with rocks to weight
Them down. Some Sabbath morn you'll float,
Your burden loosed at last, on up and up,
Your prayer book in your hand, a gift of mine,
To greet the dawn and those who make their way
To church at hours they should be sleeping." Now
The driver drew his gun, and death had been,
But quick Samoots a wristlock clamped on him,
And laid him in the street in pain.
                              "You punk!"
The driver whooped in glee to see his might
So overthrown. "I only meant to toss
A scare in you, a slug, but now I see
You're okey-doke. Yukon, he'll make it right.
He likes tough guys who slug it out with him.
They'll never say Yukon had gypped a guy
With guts. You'll hear from him, Small Fry, tonight.
Your fiddle's worth a fin. The boys will bring
A double sawbuck, maybe half a C."
But loud his helper laughed. "A Strad," he said,
"His grandpap bought. You couldn't buy Samoots
Another Strad with C's. Five G's and more
Those babies cost; don't make 'em any more.
Now lam, Samoots, before we run you down."
In haste they rumbled off past sad Samoots.
But yet that night two strangers came with word
From Yukon dread. "The boss has heard you said
You'd sink him in the drink. You'll ride with us.
He wants to see you—now." No more they spoke,
But guns they pressed against Samoots's ribs,
And drove him straight to Yukon's lair, Two Treys.
"He's here," they cried. "We bump him now,
Or take him for a ride?"

"Not him." Their chief
Beamed on Samoots. "We need some gees like him.
I'm Yukon, Bud, the guy you said you'd plant
In wet concrete, rub out, erase, I hear.
Now what's this all about?" The guns still pressed;
Yet stern Samoots no mercy sought. He leered.
"You got it right," he said. "You wanna now
Make something of it? Shoot. You've got the guns.
At 4 A.M. I'm going home today
When your gorillas knock me off my pegs
And smash the fiddle I had meant to play
Some day in Carmen. Me, I make my dough
In speaks, by pennies, Yukon. Still my time
Would one day come, except your monkeys dumb
Smash up my Strad. Now you can go to Hell.
Shoot me. I'd rather die then live without
My violin."
The gangster marked. "O.K.,
Sweetheart. I've got a spot for standup guys.
Here's fifty C's. If that won't square us up
I'll pay you well—a half a grand a month
For life. Enough for all the fiddles you
Can play. The job's a pipe. I need a guy
To plug the Gennas when they get too tough. A guy
They won't suspect. In all the speaks you're known—
A penny-cadging fiddler, nothing more.
A sawed-off shotgun you can pack sometimes
Within your case. No one would ever guess.
And when you've let 'em have it with some slugs
You drop the shotgun back inside and scram.
Is it a deal?"
"A killer, I? No soap.
I'll see my name in lights when you are dead."
So answered him Samoots.
"Don't be a sap.

With fifty C's go buy a violin,
And hire a long-haired prof to teach you tricks.
Ten years from now you'll see yourself in films—
The first to pack a gat in fiddle case.
You'll have half a grand a month for pay,
And time for practice, days on end. Old Mitch
The Snitch knows opry guys, can get you in.
And you can play for Garden."
                                    Thus Samoots
A killer 'came. For gold he sold his soul;
New violins he bought, but played no more
The joyous tunes that he had loved ere yet
He'd learned of wealth.
                              Now Heim the Fence was shot.
None saw the killer, save, perchance, a man of stature
            small
Who bore a violin. Police had wished
To talk with him; he might have had a clue.
But earth had swallowed up his form. The crime
Was written down a mystery unsolved.
Scarce dry the ink when Pinkie Sam fell dead.
"New gang assassin strikes again. Seek man
With Violin," the papers said. The law
Appealed in vain for help from him, the man
Who twice had been eye witness, fled in haste,
When gangland guns had taken life. Months passed
And years, and men still died from shotgun slugs,
And oft the papers told of fiddler shy,
A will o' wisp who hat in hand had trudged
The neighborhood the while the killer stalked
His prey. Were some who said the fiddler might
The gunman be. The law said no.
                                    One night
Samoots was pointed out within his box.
"The fiddler shy," one said. "I saw him near

The night that Boxcar Jones was tommy gunned."
But gravely shook his head the man in blue.
"A wealthy patron, friend," he said, "who comes
Each night the opera to hear in high
Silk hat, white gloves, and soup and fish. His car
Has handles all of gold. Sooner I'd suspect
My grandma, you, or Sammy Insull *père*.
A powder take, before I run you in."

The clasp of gold was turned. From out the car
The man of wealth stepped gaily, violin
Within its case beneath his arm. A nod
He gave the loungers, come by wont to see
The nightly pageant at the barber shop.
"Once over light, Joe," mocked The Little Man.
"A brighter polish on my nails, and just
A touch of brown where gray caught up with me.
My temples, Joe. Run out for some cigars,
Too, Joe, the best, three for a buck." Dark scowled
The Little Man. "They'll wizen up some time
To him. Look at him now. He sits as if
He owned that barber shop and all the town.
He's going to the opening tonight
To sit among the upper crust and smile.
I'd like to see the South Side move in."

His words are low, but now the man who drives
Samoots takes flight afoot.
                              "You'd think the mug
Had heard me then. What's up? They're here. The mob.
I'd better get down flat. O God, don't let
Them think I stooled." The Little Man falls prone
As guns begin to roar within the car

That passes by. The bullets find their mark.
Samoots is dead, beside the barber's chair.
"The Shotgun Kid!" the killers grim call back.
"You fooled us with that fiddle case too long."

CHAPTER 8

The reception lobby of the *Her-Ex* city room was like none other in the world. Here came Battling Nelson, Flagpole Sitter Joe Powers, a woman who said she was Bob Fitzsimmons' widow, superannuated members of Arctic expeditions, Senator James Hamilton Lewis, water walkers with pontoon shoes, tree sitters, pioneer nudists, and trained seal acts.

Battling Nelson handed visitors his card, with the explanation that it read Battling Nelson I to distinguish him from all the babies that had been named after him. For attractive women he would square off, shadowbox around the room, and offer to beat up anyone they didn't like, including their husbands. Flagpole Sitter Joe came seeking publicity, for he got a cut of the rental of the binoculars hawked in the Loop, the better to see him, but a colleague of his who slipped furtively in and out didn't really give a damn about flagpole sitting. He had found it was a way to keep away from process servers in his wife's divorce suit while earning some money on the side.

But Joe sat atop flagpoles for the fun of it. And he climbed the pole of the Morrison Hotel tower with the *Her-Ex*'s blessing, while Fred Pasley, the biographer of Al Capone, sat down in the lobby writing reams about him as the sidewalk entrepreneurs reaped fortunes charging customers ten cents a peep through their binoculars. Through it all, Joe refused to dignify by a reply the rumors that a blonde was hoisted up to him in the wee hours to make sure that romance did not go out of his life.

Elderly gentlemen professing to be Kidnapped Charlie Ross came occasionally. To a man they were genteel as well as amiable and rarely seemed disconcerted that we disbelieved them. Most of them said they had made modest fortunes after escaping, years after the kidnapping, from their captors. Only one that I recall ever asked for a handout, and I do not remember one who tried to sell his story to the paper. My impression was that they just wanted the *Her-Ex* to know they were safe so that we would stop worrying.

Bert Acosta came when he was in town to reminisce about his barnstorming days when his idea of fun was to knock over rows of haystacks with his plane.

James Hamilton Lewis, the most elegantly dressed senator of the century, passed through the waiting room when he visited the managing editor. The senator went for golden vests, Prince Albert coats, high hats, and spats. His whiskers were saffron, so that he resembled Yellow Kid Weil, the greatest confidence man of the day, when the Kid was dressed to impress a sucker.

Like Battling Nelson, most of our visitors had their acts. Ham Lewis's was to survey the lobby crowd, pick out the prettiest woman there, bow, doff his hat, and tell her: "Madam, I shall be honored if you will present my respects to your husband and tell him that United States Senator James Hamilton Lewis assures him that he has the most beautiful wife in Chicago."

The man we called the Self-Styled Celestial Messenger discontinued his visits and left us rather severely alone after we published some slightly uncomplimentary stories about him and his romances with the little daughters of members of his cult. But the barefoot old man in the spotless white suit, whose banner proclaimed him Jesus Christ, never seemed to weary of the place.

The nudists were generally insincere folk who hoped to land a vaudeville contract at the State-Lake Theater by getting their picture in the paper. The trained seal acts were out of work and also hoping for a picture that would get them a job, but the seals, and the girls and men who trained them, would have broken your heart. All of them were hungry.

The seals and their trainers never got hungrier at the *Her-Ex*. In a cubbyhole around the corner from the reception lobby, the part-time receptionist and his wife had a hot plate and grill on which they concocted hot dogs and hamburgers for members of the staff too busy to get out to eat. When the seals came in, the cooks fired up and made everybody something to eat. The seals didn't mind that they weren't getting fish, and the trainers loved their first meal in a week. Everybody left happy.

There were debutantes who came to confess murders they couldn't possibly have committed, elderly spinsters insisting they had been raped, a woman who said she had two children by Samuel Insull, a girl who told us that G-men had concealed invisible radio sets in her ears so that they could listen in on her innermost thoughts, and a great many washed-out blondes trying to break into the evangelism game. Why, they asked, should Aimee Semple McPherson make all the money?

When John Dillinger kicked out Polly Hamilton for The Lady in Red, who was with him when G-men ambushed and killed him, Polly came in to tell her story, not sell it. City editor Harry Read assigned me to inverview her and established us in the managing editor's office with two bottles of whisky. I had to drink with her to keep up her confidence, for she feared that Dillinger might burst in at any moment with a gun, and by the time I had finished getting her story both bottles were empty.

The girl who accused the G-men of wiring her for sound had a story of her own. The rascals, she averred, were also pumping noxious gas into her room to stupefy her and were burning her with heat rays. She had bought a device to purify the gas and a sheet of lead to protect her from the heat rays; and she had gone to Washington, she said, to complain to some members of Congress she knew, and they had showered her with money. I dismissed her as slightly nuttier than the general run, but she came back next day. Opening her purse, she showed me what she said were the congressmen's gifts—eight $1,000 bills and twenty-four $100 bills.

The burros that turned up in the reception room were my fault. I had written a story of the Chicago Black Horse Troop's need for burro racing and polo as a diversion at the military unit's polo games:

"The burro is thorough. At polo he's aces, or solo in races."

The owner of seven burros had them delivered from his stock farm to managing editor Johnnie Dienhart, each in a jaunty pair of slacks and a blazer.

During the search for the kidnapped Lindbergh baby, a serious and rather well-educated woman came into the reception room with the promise that she could track down the kidnappers and restore the child to his parents if she were placed in sole charge of the paper. How? Providence would guide her. We didn't turn the paper over to her.

A few days later I was sitting at the breakfast table in my home when another woman got into the act. The day city editor telephoned me, gave me an address, and said: "Hop over there quick. A dame just telephoned that she's got the Lindbergh baby there."

When I stepped from my cab, I was almost trampled by a mob of other reporters who began piling out of other cabs half a second later. Their offices had all received the same message. First to the door, I shouted to the housekeeper who answered my ring, "Give me the Lindbergh baby, and be quick about it!"

She smiled happily, put her fingers to her lips, and invited me in. The rest of the troop dashed in likewise, scowl though I did, because her welcome had been for me. I recognized the housekeeper as a woman who frequented the reception lobby. We found that the house was that of a woman member of the Illinois House of Representatives, who was out of town and consequently unaware of what her housekeeper was up to. The housekeeper explained why she had stood the town on its ear by telephoning the newspapers that she had the baby. She didn't exactly have him, she said. But years before, when she was a magazine subscription peddler, she had stopped in a small Illinois town. Across the street from her lodgings, she had been told, was the haunt of a ruffian gang in a lumberyard. That gang, she explained hopefully, might have kidnapped the baby. That was why she had reported the matter. It wouldn't hurt to investigate.

The characters in this strange world in which we lived weren't all screwballs. In those days people looked upon the newspaper as the court of last appeal, where they could go to get help when they needed it. A case in point was the woman who came in to ask about her cab. She had been arrested while driving six men to a picnic too fast, and the police had kept her cab. A woman cabby? Of course not, she said indignantly, and the men were her friends. The Yellow Cab Company, she explained, auctioned off its old cabs for family cars, and because they rode so comfortably she had bought one. She had to have it painted black, of course, before the company would give her title to it. We thanked her for this enlightening information on the automobile business and persuaded the police to give her back her cab.

Once in a while the Humane Hangman came in. He had begun life as a farmer in southern Illinois, and one day he chanced to get an invitation to a hanging. He was appalled at what he saw: a clumsy sheriff who never before had performed a hanging. Everything went wrong, and the condemned man dangled for five minutes until, mercifully, death came. The Humane Hangman went to more hangings and witnessed similar atrocities. He decided to study the business of hanging and volunteer his services anywhere in the country that there was to be an execution, in the days before the electric chair and the gas chamber.

When his study was complete, he performed a couple of hangings, faultlessly and painlessly, and suddenly he became the vogue among the nation's sheriffs. They were grateful for a professional in the macabre business they had often had to conduct before their terms expired. Out of deference to his family, which hated such publicity, he shoved his own name into the background and billed himself thenceforth as the Humane Hangman.

With dozens of hangings behind him now, he became a legend. Men sentenced to the rope wrote to him, asking him to do their executions. Traveling at his own expense, he made friends with those he was about to send to their death. One of them offered to commit suicide by chewing up his glass eye to spare the Humane Hangman from having to perform his grisly task.

Late in life he married. His bride thought his occasional nips were bad for him. So he built a cottage with several little trapdoor compartments in the low ceilings. Into the compartment above each trapdoor he placed a bottle. Then, when his wife was out of the room, he could reach up and pour himself a drink, without anyone ever suspecting.

CHAPTER 9

The day the Dionne quintuplets were born had been a dull one at the *Her-Ex*. Ham Lewis had been back from Washington for a week, since the spring recess of Congress, but he hadn't checked in. Dynamite, the copyboy, insisted that he had seen Charlie MacArthur on the street, and it wasn't like Charlie to forget us when he was in town.

Sam Blair stepped out after performing his daily ritual of dropping a lighted cigarette into a pile of newspapers to prove his theory that carelessly dropped cigarettes do not cause fires. He would be desolated when he returned, for a black-hearted young reporter with no respect for his elders had turned the papers into a pyre by lighting a match under them. Delos Avery hadn't been near the water cooler, where he used to lure young reporters when he had a story he didn't want to write and hand them the assignment along with one of the miniature bottles of bourbon that he always carried in his jacket pocket.

There had been a gangland bombing, and two gangsters had been shot to death. But Romy had refused to dignify them with his Boom! Boom! song on the grounds that they were small-timers. Buddy Baer had called, but only to see the goldfish that Jack Elder, the former Notre Dame football star, cultivated in a complicated system of glass tubing in Warren Brown's sports department. Buddy was a character. Far from hating Joe Louis for licking him twice, he always was singing Joe's praises because Joe had allowed him to fight him, and thus make a pot of dough in a game that was run to make it possible for everybody to make money.

The minutes ticked on toward the 4:45 P.M. deadline. The gnarled old supervising managing editor the copyboys called Dracula wondered aloud, as was his daily wont, if the *American* were scooping us. The *American* was the Hearst afternoon paper and hence, technically speaking, our sister paper. But the rivalry between us and the *American* was fantastic. Scooping that paper was like scooping the world, and the *American* felt the same way about us. Its final edition came off the presses almost at the same time as our first, or Bulldog, edition.

We were crowding our deadline when Ash De Witt, the day managing editor, approached me with some wire service copy in his hand. It was the story of the Dionne quintuplets' birth. He asked me if I had read Joe Willicombe's message on the bulletin board. I told him I had.

It was a typical telegram from Mr. Hearst's chief of staff, and it was a stern warning against the rash of multiple birth stories of the preceding weeks. Invariably, the number had been right: five, six, seven, or eight, in the wilds of Africa or on some obscure, unpronounceable island. The number was always right, but the offspring always turned out next day to be armadillos, pigs, kangaroos, penguins, or aardvarks.

"The Chief," Willicombe had wired in his never-varying allusion to Mr. Hearst, "orders that no more multiple birth stories be printed unless they are absolutely verified."

De Witt told me, when he handed me the wire copy on that blustery day in May of 1934, "Callendar is a small town. All the telephone lines have been tied up all day and we haven't been able to verify this. But we can't wait.

"I want you to boil it down into a four-head. [Two paragraphs in *Her-Ex* parlance.] Make it absolutely clear that it's only a report, completely unverified. I have to print it, but I'm going to bury it—so far inside that nobody will ever read it."

I wrote the story ever so carefully, ever so factually, ever so briefly, ever so fearsomely, for I knew that if it were true I might be working on the story of the century—and playing it down.

Then I stole across the street to the staff's favorite saloon, a converted speakeasy from the days of Prohibition, to seek advice from a fellow toiler in the vineyard. He was sipping a gin buck in memory of his last vacation of the dry era. In its last year as a speak, he had spent his entire vacation there—without ever moving out. His admiring wife brought him clean shirts and fresh suits, and the speakeasy owner let him use the shower.

"Could be the greatest," he said morosely. "And you'd be the guy who muffed it. Sally Rand's coming back to town. So's Aimee McPherson. One of them might need a press agent. And then again, maybe you won't get fired. How do you know the story isn't a phony? We fell for those armadillos. Maybe dionne is some strange creature you happen never to have heard of."

He ordered another gin buck—double.

With considerable trepidation, I awaited the first edition. There it was, buried on Page 37. Up came the *American's* final. There it was, on Page One, beneath two black lines of gigantic head type that newspapermen say the papers reserve for the Second Coming. The birth of the Quints was told in flamboyant style, and the *American's* star reporter, Charlie Blake, was flying to them with an incubator for every one.

We caught up in the next edition with our own Second Coming type. I got ready to clean out my desk on an instant's notice. But never a word was heard about the matter from Joe

Willicombe. Why, I'll never know. The editors all kept their jobs, and I kept mine.

I always wondered, though, who tied up all the telephone lines to Callendar.

It was an astute, if sleepy, editor who sent me chasing the child brides of Tennessee. He was reading the early morning wire service tickers when he came upon a paragraph that fascinated him. A Tennessee girl of thirteen was to go on trial the next Monday for murdering her husband, age fourteen.

What the editor didn't know was that child brides were forever shooting their husbands in the South at that time, and that the Southerners thought the stories would give their land a bad name. Southern papers, accordingly, didn't exactly sensationalize the killings, and the wire services, therefore, saw little news in them. It was doubtless a dull day for news when some Tennessee wire service had put the paragraph on the wire.

Airplane travel wasn't so good in those days, but by Monday noon I was in the town where Matty Pearl should have been on trial. She wasn't. The court had been so delighted by my telegraph request for space at the press table that the opening of the trial had been postponed when I failed to show up on time, lest I miss any of it. Moreover, the judge informed me proudly, there would be no difficulty getting a jury. There generally was, for the mountain folk shunned jury service. But the word of my advent had been spread, and more than 250 prospective jurors were on hand.

The defense lawyer introduced himself. He was Charles Raulston, who had won national fame years before by presiding at the Scopes evolution trial. The prosecuting attorney assured me that he was a Harvard man who always wore shoes in the Tennessee hills.

Eager for jury service in this case, when a big-city newspaper would be covering the trial, those called solemnly denied that they were kinfolk of Matty Pearl and promised the court a fair trial. Before the afternoon was over a jury of good men and true had been selected, and I went down to the jail to talk with Matty. She made no pretense of not having shot her husband. Indeed, she had painted on the wall of her cell: "Matty Pearl killed a yellow dog."

I hurried out to buy her a pair of high-heeled shoes for her bare feet and an ostentatious hat that brought out the beauty of her flaxen hair. Then I hired the town photographer to take her picture and put it in the mail, for there were no wire photo facilities available.

Matty's lawyer had laid elaborate plans to plead self-defense for her, but he hadn't reckoned with the code of the hills: when a young girl was on trial for murder, an elder relative must take the rap. And so, midway in the trial, Matty's married nineteen-year-old sister announced that she had done the shooting. This might have caused a mistrial in some jurisdictions, but not in this one. The trial proceeded, and the jury found Matty not guilty.

Members of the legal profession took me out for dinner and a drink—in a state that was then legally dry. The law proved to be no obstacle. When we wanted a drink, we merely turned our extra coffee cup upside down and it was immediately filled. Incidentally, there hadn't been any press table. The judge had moved in a desk for me, the only reporter.

Matty Pearl became the heroine of the hills. The judge told me proudly that she was the finest example of hills women marksmen. She had shot her husband through the heart with the first bullet from her rifle.

Concern for her safety was nevertheless expressed, because of The Avenger. Under the tradition of the hills, he must be a kinsman of the murder victim, whose duty it was to help the prosecution and see that justice be done in case of the defendant's acquittal. But the man who should have been The Avenger had not come forward to help press the charges against Matty. There were stories that there had been bad blood between him and the victim because the victim, in happier days, used to shoot holes in The Avenger's boat, below the waterline. At any rate, nobody ever took a potshot at Matty after her acquittal.

Now came a killer child bride emerita to bask in Matty's glory. She was a brunette of twenty-one who had shot her husband when she was a year younger than Matty and had been acquitted. But no big-city paper had covered the trial, and so she had gone down into oblivion, to be henceforth merely the widow Saunders. I wrote a story about her, and she was eternally grateful.

Before I left, the lawyers told me about another child bride murder trial coming up in a not too distant county. I determined to cover it if my editors agreed.

Agreed? They were jubilant when I got back to Chicago, for Matty's story had brought in readers' compliments by the hundreds. It was something fresh in a city whose daily reading had been gangland bombings and shootings. A sociologist at the University of Chicago wanted my information for a book.

Off I went to Tennessee to cover the next trial, and the next, and the next. Usually I returned with a suitcase full of moonshine, confiscated by the sheriff and turned over to deserving politicians.

Kenesaw Mountain Landis, first baseball commissioner and nemesis of the malefactors in the Chicago White Sox scandal (CHICAGO TRIBUNE)

Mustachioed Diamond Jim Colosimo, surrounded by his family and friends (CHICAGO TRIBUNE)

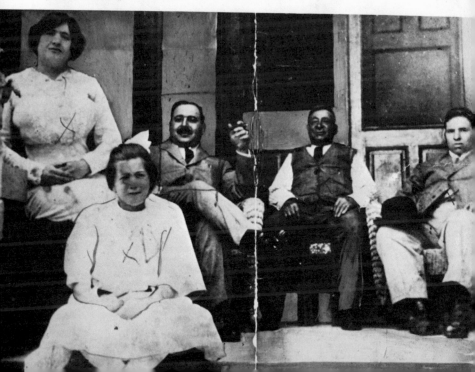

Dale Winter, the choir singer who later married Diamond Jim Colosimo, and after his murder starred in the musical comedy *Irene* (CHICAGO TRIBUNE)

Colosimo's restaurant, haunt of opera stars and society (CHICAGO TRIBUNE)

Colosimo's restaurant, with funeral cortege in front as it paused, with two bands playing, to do a funeral dirge for Diamond Jim (CHICAGO TODAY)

Clarence Darrow, left, and William Jennings Bryan at the Tennessee evolution trial (CHICAGO TRIBUNE)

Chicago's Greeter George D. Gaw, resplendent in white (CHICAGO TRIBUNE)

Al Capone, king of Chicago's gangland (CHICAGO TRIBUNE)

Irene Castle McLaughlin, celebrated dancing partner of Vernon Castle and later a crusader against medical school vivisection of dogs (CHICAGO TRIBUNE)

James Hamilton Lewis when a senator from Illinois and a flatterer of beautiful women (CHICAGO TRIBUNE)

Battling Nelson, prizefighter and loquacious defender of women (CHICAGO TRIBUNE)

John Scopes,
who refused to pose as a monkey
(CHICAGO TRIBUNE)

Eugene McDonald, head of Zenith (wearing a hat) and man-about-town
(CHICAGO TRIBUNE)

Sally Rand with the fan that made her famous (CHICAGO TRIBUNE)

CHAPTER 10

The *Her-Ex* had great editors. But it had greater copyboys—Dynamite, Mickie, Frank, Charlie, Mitchie, Chester, Bob, Shorty, Al, Van, and during my years scores of other freckle-faced urchins who shortchanged us when we sent them for sandwiches and who called the managing editor by his first name. The editors were virtually unerring in their judgment of news; the copyboys were completely so. They read our copy as they snailed it over to the city desk, damning it with a yawn or approving it with a chuckle. When they laughed aloud, it was headed for Page One. When they returned to say, with tolerant impudence, that they hadn't quite got the point, it was certain to come back from the man in the slot with a request that it be rewritten from a different angle.

The rewrite man who slighted a copyboy paid for his transgression. By a slip, the rewriter could make a boo-boo that could lay the paper open to a million-dollar libel suit. And the copyboys, who caught things like that by instinct before they slipped past the editors, would say nothing about it. The rewrite men were aware of this and treated the copyboys with respect, whether the rewriters owed them a dollar or not. They might want to borrow one on Thursday.

Consider Dynamite. The name is not of my manufacture. That is actually what they called him. He wore his hair in his eyes and knew more about the paper than the publisher did. If you wanted a raise, theater tickets, a boat trip on the Great Lakes, or airplane transportation gratis, you saw Dynamite. He could get you an extra day off, have your hours changed, or adjust your income tax problems. We all confidently expected that some day we should be working for him. (He later became a Chicago public relations tycoon.)

A grateful rewrite staff turned out masterpieces of literature for him which astounded his English composition teachers. When he was graduated from high school he tried to get the school authorities to inscribe his diploma to him and the *Her-Ex* rewriters.

At seventeen he was writing his memoirs. He had eaten the mayor's steak at the banquet that welcomed Lindbergh back from Paris and, doubtless, had thumbed his nose at governors in his capacity as confidant to the editors.

Chester was the terror of the editors. He never liked the way they put the paper out and told them so. Eventually he became so domineering that they had to give him a promotion to reporter—the old *Her-Ex* game of kicking them upstairs.

Bob was Chester's brother. He criticized the staff as well as the editors, tipped off newcomers as to what the managing editor didn't like, and straightened out family difficulties, until his knowledge of everyone's affairs became too embarrassing. He had to be kicked upstairs too.

Hank wasn't there long enough for anyone to get his last name. On his first day, which was his last, he approached the editor the copyboys called Dracula with some proofs and inquired, "Who's this guy Dracula?"

Charlie had scant regard for the mentality of rewrite men and editors. No one should have been surprised, therefore, when he arched his eyebrows the night Ash De Witt gave him $20 with instructions to put it on the nose of a horse that Charlie figured couldn't run for sour apples. Something of a handicapper himself, Charlie checked over the Racing Form again to be sure.

And then, honest to the core but a trifle superior withal, he dropped the money into his own pocket, smiling as he contemplated how pleased his boss would be after the race next day to get his money back with the explanation that it hadn't been lost after all.

The thing Charlie didn't know was that the boss happened to have a genuine tip from its owner that the horse was going to win. The odds were fabulous. Everyone thought that Charlie never would come back. He did, though, received the boss's forgiveness, and two years later he had his own handicapping column on the races.

Frank was perhaps the dumbest copyboy I had ever known. He would forget what he had been sent to do in the middle of an errand. Geniuses are that way. One night the composing room needed some new filler copy. Since the copyreaders were all busy, Frank sat down, selected some filler, and wrote over it some heads that sparkled. They took him off the copyboy payroll and made him a copyreader, and Frank, a trifle bewildered by it all, made good. Like that!

Copyboys were extraordinarily successful at playing the Printers' Pool. This was an undercover lottery in which printers and newspaper folk all over the city invested a dollar a week. Each investor had a number that he was entitled to keep permanently. But quite often a number holder, discouraged by years of never hitting the jackpot, would sell his number to a copyboy, and that very week, it seemed, the number would come up, paying the boy $100, $500, or even the top prize of $1,000.

Harry Munzell, perennial secretary to the ever coming and going managing editors, finally gave up his number in disgust, turning it over to a reporter, who changed his mind and turned it over to a copyboy. The first week it paid him $1,000. Thinking it was a once-in-a-lifetime shot, the copyboy in turn relinquished the number to another copyboy. Unhappily, Munzell saw the second copyboy win $500 with his old number.

Copyboys, who came on the run at the call of "Boyee! Copee!" to carry the copy from the rewriters to the city desk and run all manner of errands in between, began vanishing from the scene with the coming of World War II. In their place came copygirls, college graduates hoping to break into the newspaper business and journalism students in campus finery, determined to find out all about newspapers first hand. Another grand old institution has gone.

The husband and wife who ran the hot dog and hamburger business in the cubbyhole adjoining the reception lobby had to go out of business when a man died from meningitis and the health department said their sandwiches might have been responsible. This brought on a crisis, for the hard-working copyboys sometimes didn't have time to go downstairs to DeMet's restaurant to bring us a snack when we were hungry.

The departure from the scene of the husband and wife team of amateur restaurateurs led to the establishment of the Gallery of Strangers, the weirdest assemblage I have ever seen. The Gallery members sat on a long, elevated bench, ready to run errands on a moment's notice. The charter member was a little Filipino busboy from DeMet's, where necessity had forced us to order sandwiches by telephone. He fell in love with us at first sight and soon was bringing us fifty-cent sandwiches for forty cents and stealing us desserts. Discovering that we were generous tippers, he quit his job and moved into the city room to run errands for us and subsist on our tips.

Presently he was joined by Tony, a half-starved little Italian boy who stole through the side door one day and became the official shoe shiner. So long as there were shoes to shine or errands to run, Tony remained, sometimes departing wearily for home as late as ten at night, invariably carrying home with him an armload of old papers.

The papers aroused the curiosity of Earl Aykroid, an assistant city editor, who finally asked Tony why he lugged them home. Tony, it turned out, was the eldest of nine children whose mother had a hard time feeding them because their father was paralyzed. He carried the papers home because they could be used as protection against the cold in their ill-heated flat.

The kindest-hearted slobs in the newspaper world set to work to remedy conditions by getting shines they didn't need and overtipping Tony. When his birthday rolled around, Delos Avery bought him a suit of clothes. One of the editors contributed an overcoat his son had outgrown. Everybody tossed in money. Tony got, in addition, a basketball, gym suit, boxing gloves, and even an old set of golf clubs.

When he announced his upcoming birthday again, the generosity increased, for the little shoe shiner had begun telling appalling stories of the misfortunes of his family while he sweated out his hours after school trying to feed the brood. Nothing was too good for him and his family this time. Plans for a third birthday drive were progressing merrily when someone happened to remember: Tony had been with us only a few months.

When we realized that we had been turning Tony into a juvenile racketeer with our generosity, we called him in and explained the American way of life to him. He reformed and from that day on accepted no gifts, but worked for what he got. Charity? He'd have spit in your eye.

Now a taxicab driver joined up, to become, with the Filipino and Tony, the nucleus of our Gallery. He was a roly-poly little man named Zeke, but we called him Little Romy because of his remarkable resemblance, except in stature, to Romy. He was even shorter.

Little Romy first came into the city room to deliver some picture plates for a photographer. His fascination was so great that he stayed an hour. Next day he came back for a visit, and since Carlos, the Filipino waiter, and Tony were busy running to the restaurant and drugstore for food for the ever hungry staff, Little Romy cut in on the tips by running some errands himself. The next day he just abandoned his cab out in front and became a permanent member of the Gallery.

The growth of the Gallery might have ended there had not Chicago's mayor, Anton J. Cermak, been shot by an assassin gunning for President-elect Franklin D. Roosevelt at Miami. A deathwatch was set up at once in our office and also in Miami, where Johnnie Dienhart, the mayor's close friend, was in charge. For nineteen nights we kept a full complement of rewrite men on the job all night, ready for the moment we knew would come.

With nothing whatever to do in the long hours after midnight, when the restaurant and drugstore were closed, the Gallery members took to playing poker, and reporters who should have gone home remained to join in the fun. The Gallery members couldn't tear themselves away from the excitement. Now they were joined by Peanuts, a Hungarian who peddled peanuts, candy bars, and fruits throughout the building when he wasn't lamenting that we called him Peanuts and poked fun at him despite his claim that he held a degree from a university in the old country. He learned to play poker and told himself his working days were over, except for running errands for tips.

Peanuts was the day vendor to the building, and he was violating a gentlemen's agreement with the night vendor by being around, for any purpose, at night. The night vendor was a great, hulking Slav, although the women reporters insisted that he had the eyes of a poet. When his remonstrances failed to get Peanuts off his chronological territory, the night vendor put aside his basket of fruits and nuts and joined the gambling group himself.

One night the flash came. Mayor Cermak was dead. We tore up the paper and filled it with a precooked obituary, a review of the shooting, and dozens of hastily written stories under Miami datelines. Next day the glamor was all gone. Things settled back to their old routine. Peanuts discovered that he couldn't cash the I.O.U.'s he had won at poker and moodily returned to his peddling. The man with the eyes of a poet left in disillusionment and was never seen again. The cabdriver, having had his day in the sun, lost interest in the relatively drab events of the letdown and resumed his cab driving. The waiter remained, for the *Her-Ex* folk were always hungry enough to send him downstairs for sandwiches. Tony, the once underfed and emaciated little Italian bootblack, became so beefy from the meat the staff's tips provided him that he embarked on a career as a prizefighter.

Mayor Cermak's death provided a scoop, through one of the strange twists of the newspaper game, but not for us. The deathwatch reporters at Miami had for nights been lined up on a fence outside the hospital for their nightly vigil. One of the physicians was to let them know when the mayor died by pulling down the shade of a hospital window.

It was a boring time, and flasks were broken out. One night somebody suggested that they all run down to the nearest saloon for a quick drink with ice in it. If anything happened, they reasoned, nobody could be scooped because they would all miss it and recover together. Down to the drinking spot they ran. But not all.

One of their number had slipped unnoticed from his perch on the fence and had fallen asleep. What awakened him nobody will ever know. But he suddenly snapped to and pulled himself up from behind the fence. At that very moment the shade went down. Racing to a telephone, with many an imprecation for his comrades for deserting him—to justify his determination to scoop them—he flashed the news to his paper. The rest learned that the mayor had died when they returned twenty minutes later.

The story recalls another, which some say is apocryphal and others insist is true, of a premature flash on the death of President Harding in San Francisco.

One of the reporters traveling with the President, as the tale goes, became so worn out that he abandoned his vigil and fell asleep. He dreamed that Mr. Harding had died, and the dream was so realistic that, in a sort of dream-world stupor, he telephoned a story of the President's death to his paper, two thousand miles away. The wayward correspondent was saved when Harding actually died.

Arthur Brisbane was our god on the *Her-Ex*. His thundering editorials ran on our front page and on the front pages of Hearst papers throughout the land under the heading "Today." His writings would be regarded as fundamentalist these days, for he wove into them all the moral ethics of the Bible Belt and William Jennings Bryan. He rewrote history, mythology, and science to fit his theories. His editorials were unadulterated corn, devoid of humor, but the corn was written in a polished, Harvard-type style, or that of Gilbert and Sullivan.

Brisbane never was a man to laugh heartily at himself. We all remembered the stubborn war he had carried on against Westbrook Pegler over a column Pegler had written burlesquing his style and ideas. There was, too, the story of some wag —some believed it was Rube Goldberg and some credited it to Gene Fowler—who once jumped into Brisbane's parked automobile in New York and dictated a facetious Arthur Brisbane column into the recording machine that Brisbane always kept with him. The column got on the wire, and for years, it was said, Brisbane carried on a relentless campaign to find out who did it and to have him punished.

An even more recent event should have given me warning when I was asked to beard the lion in his den. There was at the time a millionaire girl who had sued her aunt, charging that the aunt had had her sterilized. The story had been on all the front pages. Fun-loving Gene Fowler had told the story in a long poem entitled "The Sterilized Heiress," a hilarious epic parodying the Brisbane manner and intended strictly for the entertainment of the managing editors. Indeed, when it was put on the Hearst wires, it was marked personal and confidential to managing editors. But the poem was leaked, and presently everyone interested in that sort of thing had a copy. Brisbane burned.

It was with this background that I got into the picture, and almost out of the Hearst empire.

Our publisher, Homer Guck, was coming home from the hospital. A special edition memorializing his return was decreed—a limited edition intended for Guck and the editors, with perhaps a few copies for the Hearst headquarters in New York. Selected members of the staff were asked to contribute something gay and frivolous honoring Guck.

Rather casually, I was told to write a Brisbane column. With never a thought of the consequences, I turned out one that the editors didn't bother to read, because they thought it would be innocuous. When they saw it in print, they were frightened half out of their wits. When they realized how far out on a limb I had put them, they sent a hundred copies to Guck, each took one for himself, and destroyed the rest. None ever got to New York.

The column was almost accidental. I began somewhat disinterestedly to write it and found myself enjoying the task. Victor Barnes, who read copy on the column, chuckled over the first paragraph. That was all I needed. I wrote:

Homer Guck, wise citizen, will be out of the hospital today. Five hundred thousand years ago, when this country was covered by a glacier, he would not have come out. He would have stayed in where it was warm. Man progresses. Glaciers melt.

Mr. Guck will find many changes when he steps out again on terra firma, as the ancients called this ground we walk upon. Mighty airplanes now fly higher than the clouds. New license plates have been attached to man-made machines that race over the land. That will interest Mr. Guck.

At this moment, new calendars are hanging on the walls throughout this great country. You may not have noticed when they were put up. That was January 1, celebrated in many parts of the globe as New Year's.

There have been 1933 New Years, if you are American. There have been just as many if you are Chinese. But time seems longer in China. There, time is Confucian. It is confusing to us of the Western world, at least. Not to the Chinese.

Mr. Guck noticed when the new calendar was put up. He probably did not celebrate New Year's. Modern man does not enjoy hospitals. He prefers to get out where cracked ice is plentiful. Pithecanthropus Erectus, who lived here in the glacial age, could have had a whole glacier. He would have preferred to stay inside, where there was no ice.

Pithecanthropus Erectus could not have published a newspaper. Wise Nature intended that he should be a good feature story. But editors of his time did not know that the world is interested in natural history.

At the time this is being written, editors everywhere are looking for a good story. Deadline time is approaching and nothing has happened. Mr. Guck will smile at this.

Within a very few hours, he will be making news, leaving the hospital and going home. Then he will say to his editors, in journalism's quaint language: "I scooped you. I made news. I left the hospital."

They will show him a whole edition proving him wrong. Editors are alert. Otherwise, Mr. Guck would be right.

Mr. Guck bears a name that was famous in ancient Greece. It is Homer. Homer was the man who swam the Hellespont. He could have done more for the world writing a good book, like the Odyssey. But swimming the Hellespont was worth while. It developed his muscles. Johnny Weismuller could have swum it faster and collected from the movies. There were no movies in Homer's time.

Mr. Guck will not get to see the automobile show. That is not because there are no tickets. Shrewd automobile manufacturers send newspaper publishers tickets gratis. You should be a newspaperman. Everyone should buy an automobile. Everyone should run a newspaper. That way, every newspaper publisher would have a car.

If Mr. Guck could go to the automobile show, he would find many things to think about. Thinking develops the mind. He might also get a new car. Every day someone gets a new car by taking a souvenir key presented at the automobile show to the Stevens hotel. If the key fits the car at the hotel, the fortunate gentleman gets the car.

Not everyone gets a car. Mr. Guck will be surer of one if he buys it. The other way is chance. Gamblers depend on chance. Some become wealthy, but poverty is better than wealth acquired that way, if you like poverty.

Mr. Guck will not miss the Walkathon. That began before he became ill, and will last longer. There will also be tickets for it. These are known to newspapermen as ducats. Some call them Annie Oakleys. Theater owners should give more tickets to newspapermen.

In Seattle, a man bites a dog. That's booze. He thought it was a redhot. It is tradition in newspaper offices throughout the land that it's news to bite a dog. Yet editors, who make news, do not bite dogs. The Seattle man was no editor. Neither was the dog.

In Chicago, gangsters offer $20,000 for killing a rival. These are bad times for gangsters. The gentleman upon whose head the price has been set can make money taking himself for a ride. He probably will not do it. Grasping government would send him to the penitentiary for not paying his income tax.

Scarface Al Capone would not say $20,000. Gangsters call it Twenty Grand. That is why gangsters could not be editors. Editors know their readers would confuse it with the horse.

CHAPTER 11

"New trained seal," a copyboy told me when I came into the office one afternoon. He nodded to the day city editor. I never had seen the man before, but that did not disturb me. City editors became managing editors overnight, and the managing editors about whom I write were forever swapping jobs. There was a classic gag around the *Her-Ex:* "Q—Who's your managing editor? A—I don't know. I just got back from lunch."

"A trained seal?" I asked, looking again to see if the man in the slot were bouncing a ball on his nose. "Yeah," the urchin explained, "like Damon Runyon, George McManus, or Rube Goldberg."

The trained seal turned out to be James Irwin, a crusader who had won fame as the Boy City Editor of Wisconsin. Once he had made himself a reputation, he was as vital to Mr. Hearst and the *Her-Ex* as the Graf Zeppelin, Walter Winchell, the Abominable Snowman, or a feature series by Pithecanthropus Erectus. Mr. Hearst and his *Her-Ex* editors knew they must have him the moment they heard about him. Must! Pay him anything you have to before somebody else grabs him. You can always force him to break his contract by putting him on the dogwatch writing obits.

What though his experience was only in the hinterlands on a small-town paper, he was coming to be a top boss of the brawlingest, goddamnedest big-city paper in America! He was the very man for day city editor. Into the slot he went, and God give him a loud voice.

God gave him something better—guts. By the end of the second day he was telling off the managing editor and out-Her-Exing the *Her-Ex*.

The boy city editor lasted a long time until he finally became a legend in what came to be known as the Jim Irwin-Jack Malloy test. Malloy, a long-time city editor who rose to a directorship in the Hearst empire, had become irked at the current managing editor, T.V. (Thanatopsis Virgil, so help me) Rank. Storming into Rank's office, Malloy announced his resignation. "Now, my boy, just a minute," said Rank, who knew a good man when he saw one. "Let's talk this over." He wound up persuading Malloy to stay by raising his salary.

Irwin had heard the story, and so he tried it. Storming into Rank's office, he announced his resignation. "Now, my boy," said the imperturbable Rank, "let's talk this over. You said you are resigning? Good. That's just what I was hoping you said."

The boy city editor left the *Her-Ex* precipitously. But he went on to become one of the highest-paid New York publicity experts in the business.

Even in his earliest days on the paper, he was tremendous.

"The Supreme Court has just ruled in the John T. Scopes evolution [monkey] case," he told me. "Scopes is teaching geology at the University of Chicago. Interview him and make him pose for a picture hanging from a tree like a monkey. Hands behind his back. You know! Don't bother about Clarence Darrow. I'll handle him."

My wife, Eloise, could have stopped brash young Mr. Irwin in his tracks if William Jennings Bryan hadn't passed to his reward shortly after the celebrated Tennessee evolution trial in which he and Darrow were the prima donnas. She could have told Irwin, quite truthfully, "Don't bother about William Jennings Bryan. I'll handle him. He's my great-great-uncle."

The university was then so conservative in regard to publicity that newspaper photographers had to sneak coeds off campus in order to photograph them. Henry Justin Smith had just come from his post of managing editor of the Chicago *Daily News* to be the university's public relations counselor. ("And don't call me a press agent.") Everybody was stuffy until a later president, Robert Maynard Hutchins, and a later public relations counselor, William Morgenstern, put a little hoopla into the university's press agentry.

But the university's gray towers and grayer beards couldn't daunt the boy city editor. He wanted Scopes pretending to be a monkey. Scopes wouldn't go for it. As a Tennessee public school teacher slipping a little evolution into his teachings, he had been the soul of decorum at his trial, while Darrow and Bryan took potshots at each other. His demeanor never changed, even when his defender, Darrow, called the presiding judge stupid, and then, when the judge threatened him with a contempt of court citation unless he apologized, wisecracked, "I said the judge is stupid and I'm sorry." Bryan, Scopes's prosecutor, realized that Darrow was only lampooning the judge further with the apology, but the judge, impressed at being in such fast legal company as Darrow and Bryan, happily accepted the double entendre apology.

Scopes tried to run when he saw my photographer. Under no circumstances, he said, would he pose as a monkey. The best we could get was a photograph of him at his teacher's desk, looking contrite as befitted a man who had been found guilty of the heinous crime of teaching evolution.

Evolution was a hot subject in those days, when Gallagher and Shean were bringing down the houses with, "They say Darwin's book is bunk, and their grandpap was no monk — absolutely, Mr. Gallagher; positively, Mr. Shean."

President Ernest De Witt Burton of the university died, and Max Mason came from the University of Wisconsin to take his place.

"I know that guy," the boy city editor told me. "I know that guy. He's a pool shark. Make him pose in the Quadrangle Club [the faculty drinking spot] with a pool cue in his hands. Have him pose with Michelson [Dr. Albert A. Michelson], and don't come near me until you get them shooting a game of pool."

Mason would have done it, too, if the university's pall of gloom hadn't closed in on him. He was the kind of fellow the irreverent photographers called Boss—a standup guy. I can see him now in his scholar's gown, laying the cornerstone of a new building, with an impudent *Her-Ex* cameraman, Dave Mann, calling out to him through the austere silence:

"Hey, Max! Pick up your trowel again. And a great big smile. Now just one more, Maxie."

Max did it. Certainly he did. *Her-Ex* photographers, brashest in the world, always got what they wanted when they prattled:

"Get back on the steps like you was just getting off the train, Mr. Coolidge." Or:

"Fan yourself, Queen Marie. You think Chicago's too hot. Get it?" Or:

"Hey, Madam Perkins, let's see a little more of your leg! That's it. Just a little higher now. And that old smile."

A big man in the university got himself shot. By a vandal, he said, while protecting the honor of a girl in the street. I believed it. Everyone did except Jack Malloy, the city editor at the time.

"Nuts!" he told me in that Jack Malloy tone that left you wondering whether you were fired or not. "He was in a university building with some dame when her regular boy friend caught up with them. You fell down on the story."

I began checking up. The university began clamming up and cracking down on me. Friends came around reminding me that I was an enrolled student, and maybe I'd better lay off. The university hailed the gun victim as a hero. He was an alumnus as well as an official, almost entitled to a mention in the "Alma Mater" as an ex-football hero. The "Alma Mater" was a song they sang when they lost a football game, in the days when Coach Amos Alonzo Stagg's men rarely lost.

My lifetime belief that Jack Malloy had second sight gained some confirmation years later, long too late for a scoop, when a university official with whom I was riding downtown on the Illinois Central recalled the case. "Ricochet," he said in that quarter of a second you sometimes talk before you begin to think. "You know," he said, "the bullet hole's still up there in Mitchell Tower. . . . Good God, you're not going to revive this, are you?"

When I gave up my job as campus correspondent and police reporter for an inside job, I ended the most lucrative period of my early career, the only era in which I could afford tailor-made suits, for I was paid three dollars an assignment, even though I might work only ten minutes on each and the assignments came thick and fast.

Inside I would get only forty dollars a week, and have difficulty raising the tuition for my classes at the university. No more tailored suits. But here was an opportunity to win recognition from the editors, which was more important than trying to keep up with the expensively dressed brothers of the fraternity. I couldn't keep up anyway, for they all had sleek sports roadsters.

Duffy Cornell, the man whose diabetes made it difficult for him to stay on the phone as ordered to do, in *The Front Page,* had just become city editor. Seeing a new face, he called me over and solemnly abjured me not to stay in the newspaper business. No future, he said. And then, his fatherly duty done, he sent me across the street to place a horse bet for him and buy him some of his favorite Home Run cigarettes, a brand so strong that someone else's smoke could make you sick.

One Sunday morning Romy inducted me into his own private life as a public official. He was in public service up to the neck; he was Birger of the deputy's office when he was demanding information to which he had no right from a timid citizen at the other end of the line. As Birger, he could shout threats to bring the timid citizen in via a squad car if the timid citizen seemed reluctant to discuss his private affairs by telephone. No one ever thought to ask Romy, "Deputy what?"

He sent me that morning to get a picture of a man who had been shot to death in a gangland battle. "Tell his wife you're the deputy coroner," Romy commanded, oblivious of the fact that I looked more like Joe College than a hardened public official.

The deputy had been there. So had numerous reporters insisting, to the last man, that they were the deputy coroner. The woman invited me in pleasantly, then planted herself in front of the door so that I would have to use force and risk getting myself into a legal jam to break out, and told her daughter to call the police. When I finally talked my way out with the old working my way through college as a reporter routine, which appealed to the daughter, I called Romy, approximately ten years older than when I entered the house. He laughed:

"I was afraid you didn't look the part," he confessed. "But what could I lose?"

Romy, unfortunately, wasn't the kind of man to give up. He was bland as ever when he told me one midnight of a young man who had reported his sweetheart had been kidnapped from his car in a lovers' lane. "Get out there," said Romy. "Tell 'em you're a detective and make the janitor give you the key to her room. Get her picture. Get all the pictures so there won't be any for the other papers."

I went. Flashing my white star Phi Gamma Delta pledge pin at the janitor, I proclaimed myself a police detective.

To my astonishment, and considerable relief, it worked. "I could tell you was a dick," said the janitor, pressing the key into my hand and gazing awestricken at the pledge pin in my lapel.

It was a warm summer evening. The girl was there, sleeping peacefully on her bed. No nightie. She beamed happily when I awakened her. "I wasn't kidnapped," she said. "He wanted to get out of marrying me and I jumped out of his car."

It all puzzled even Romy. He had the police question the young man, who admitted her story was true. Afraid that something might happen to the girl and he would be blamed, he had tried to prepare himself an alibi by reporting that she had been kidnapped.

Eddie Hafferkamp told me I was fired when I telephoned him a few days later for my assignments. Why? Eddie seemed perturbed that I should expect a reason for so trivial a thing. I was just fired. That was all. Lopped from the payroll. Off to the breadline. Did a *Her-Ex* reporter need a reason? Well, he said, Red Cullen had come back to the job I had inherited, but Eddie obviously hoped I wouldn't fall for that explanation. The scrambled eggs at the Harrison Orange Huts, he told me comfortingly, were quite nourishing and cheap.

Back I went to work, however, a short time later. Why? Well, that was testing the patience of even Eddie. "Forget it," he said. "You're on the payroll again." It seemed a short answer, but it was a good one. It was, I was to learn, the *Her-Ex* answer for everything. "Forget it," or "Never mind." If the editors changed their minds about sending you on an expedition to the North Pole, or advancing you from copyboy to publisher, they just told you to forget it. See? Never mind. I never did find out why I was fired, but years later I learned why I had been hired back.

CHAPTER 12

I should tell it of Walter Howey, were it not that the partisans of Frank Carson might feel slighted; tell it of Mr. Carson if Mr. Howey's followers would not think I had deliberately taken one of the great traditions away from him: the story of the rattlesnake and the cobra. Because the incident occurred before I was given an inside job at the office, I must tell it as it was told to me by the Howey worshipers, who credited it fanatically to their hero, and by the Carson partisans, who were just as insistent that their hero was in on it.

There was, at any rate, a managing editor who thought the cobra was the fightingest snake of all. And then there was Bill Hallowell, a Southern gentleman who upheld the honor of the rattler. Everyone concerned had seen the film classic of the battle between a cobra and a mongoose, which was the rage of the year. Hallowell and Howey, or Carson, made a bet. Each sent to a naturalist friend for his favorite brand of snake. The champions were placed in training for a fight to the death. It was to take place in the wee hours of the morning, after the final edition had gone to press.

The cobra, however, got out of its cage. Those who knew about it lived in fear and trembling while a desperate search was made of the building. But the snake could not be found. Jitters seized the staff. Everyone hurried down to Walgreen's drugstore on the first floor and bought a baseball bat, and soon there was a bat beside every desk. The newspaper folk saw the cobra everywhere, in the paper on the floor, behind the desks, in the wastebaskets. And then, when the management was trying to decide whether to order straightjackets for everyone or abandon the building, Peggy Doyle, the Little Girl Reporter, got a telephone call from Mayor William Hale (Big Bill) Thompson.

She was chatting with the mayor from a telephone booth when she chanced to notice movement at the top of a ventilating pipe that ran downward through the booth. The cobra was slithering down the pipe. Peggy had her baseball bat with her. She didn't scream. She just bashed the cobra's head in, said goodbye to the mayor, and walked out to assure her colleagues that their lives were in danger no more.

Another tale was that of Babe Meigs's coming to the paper as publisher. A city editor who shall be nameless was chosen toastmaster of the welcoming banquet. But, as the story was told, the toastmaster collapsed, from overwork, some said at the bar, before it was time to introduce the guest of honor. Meigs overlooked the situation and made his speech of acceptance unintroduced. As he sat down, the city editor, awakened at the applause, rose to his feet, and said triumphantly, if a trifle late, "It is now my pleasure to introduce Mr. Merrill C. Meigs, our new publisher. Let's give him a big hand."

One city editor, who later rose to the heights in the Hearst organization, began his career as a sportswriter assigned to travel with the Chicago Cubs. But he fell from the water wagon, and his stories ceased coming in. For a month the sports editor had men searching for him to tell him he was fired. Then one day he bobbed up in New York.

"I'm here, all right," he wired the sports editor. "But you've sent me the wrong team—the White Sox."

Strange things happened in Prohibition days. Homeward bound and slightly thirsty, Ash De Witt stopped at a speakeasy frequented by Checker Cab drivers. For no reason at all, he looked at the drivers assembled at the bar and blandly announced, "All Checker drivers are bastards."

When he regained consciousness, he blinked up at the man who had swung the K.O. punch, observing, in gentle reproof, "I thought we were all gentlemen here."

There was one man on the *Her-Ex* whom the editors valued above the very presses. He was a red-faced, white-haired, taciturn man of mystery from the Circulation Department who slipped in about an hour after midnight with the earliest available copy of the rival *Tribune*'s One-Star Final edition. From the first, I was convinced that Pinkie didn't worm himself into the opposition's pressroom and steal the first paper off the presses. It was clear to me that he had made a deal with a red-faced opposite number on the other paper, and that the two met by prearrangement halfway across the Loop to trade papers and scurry back to their own offices. This I was never able to prove, but if I were correct all this mysterious hanky-panky went for naught, since the papers would have been in precisely the same relative position even if they had got each other's final edition fifteen minutes later from the newsstands.

Be that as it may, the editors' reaction to the advance copy was quite the reverse of what you might have expected. If we had been scooped, they smiled happily, lifted the opposition's story and went blithely home, leaving the lobster trick man in charge. But if we hadn't, they fretted. They chewed the ends completely off their cigars and, on occasion, swallowed what was left. They knew, then, that the masterminds of the opposition had an exclusive story that they would slap in a replated

Page One the moment we were lulled into a false sense of security. The copy Pinkie had brought in was obviously a phony. A few hundred of the phony edition would be run off and then the *Tribune* would be out with its scoop. The editors were certain of it.

Pinkie would be sent out again, looking infinitely more mysterious, if he knew what was good for him. All night, until breakfast time, he would be returning with later papers. The editors wouldn't go home.

Ash De Witt was the best of the cigar chewers and by all odds the loudest voiced of the editors. When the One-Star Final was a Simon pure one that De Witt himself couldn't suspect of being a phony, he would ofttimes announce that we should put our line or eight-column banner on the story that the *Tribune* was playing. Half a dozen yes-men would enthusiastically agree.

Then lightning would flash from De Witt's eyes, and he would roar, "But, goddammit, why should we?" And half a dozen yes-men would solemnly shake their heads. Why indeed?

De Witt was a fiery editor whose fire cost him a million dollars.

After he left the *Her-Ex,* he went to Washington to become managing editor of Eleanor (Cissy) Patterson's *Times-Herald.* There he had innumerable scraps with Mrs. Patterson, who had considerable fire herself, and, when the battle became too hot, he would resign. But Mrs. Patterson had tremendous respect for him, and she always hired him back.

He had quit again when she made her last will, giving the paper upon her death to a handful of her top executives. De Witt would have been one of them, but she left him out because he wasn't working for her at the time. She died before he had decided to come back, and his delay cost him his share. The bequests to the others were estimated at considerably more than a million dollars each.

Theatrical folk who came to worship or get married in the

Little Church at the End of the Road, or to plant flowers in its garden, knew the pastor as Friar Tuck. He was Irwin St. John Tucker, day head of the copydesk, a poet as well, a liberal of the liberals, and a two-fisted minister who could tell an off-color story or, on occasion, toss off a drink with the boys.

A man of varied talents, he was counselor to Chicago's Indians, a post in which he worked wonders with the noble Wabash Avenue red men, who lived by hiring themselves out as scenery for outdoor shows. A linguist of rare accomplishment also, Friar Tuck met with some success in teaching the city Indians their native tongues, but he never had much to say of his efforts to teach his third-generation Chicago charges of the Loop primeval to handle a canoe. They were forever having to be rescued from drowning in the Chicago River.

The good friar saw no ethical bar to sneering slightly at capitalism while earning an extra living on a paper that was one of capitalism's staunchest defenders. Carrying it all a step further, he found nothing inconsistent in using the paper's time and facilities to strike a few blows for the underdog. And so he wrote an attack upon much of what the paper stood for and had it set in type in the *Her-Ex* composing room at the paper's expense, and then had the pressmen run off voluminous copies, which he distributed. Happy admirers of Friar Tuck listened to his philosophy and departed to establish a commune on an abandoned Mississippi plantation. They returned shortly, convinced that God really didn't provide, as Friar Tuck had told them, or that the good friar had been talking through his hat.

The death of Arthur Brisbane, bellwether of the Hearst writers, might well have been one of the great moments of the *Her-Ex*. Instead, it was one of its fiascos. Brisbane died early on Christmas morning in 1936. As I hiked across the Loop in the darkness to begin work on the early edition, the *Tribune* was selling extras with the story of his death. There was no *Her-Ex* extra. I learned why when I reached the office. The last of the printers had been allowed to go home early, because it was Christmas, just before the word of Brisbane's death came in. He was our ace, but we couldn't tell the world he was gone. His last column was running in the morning edition.

CHAPTER 13

The Great Depression struck the *Her-Ex* without warning. True, my wife and I had heard rumblings of trouble when we were returning home from our honeymoon in Europe. But we knew that nothing disastrous could happen to the United States. Not in the year 1929.

Nevertheless, the stock market crashed on October 29. Soon our friends outside the newspaper business were out of work. The nation was out of work. Factories closed. All over the country, huge apartment buildings were left unfinished, their stark walls standing as a reminder of what in those days, but not now, everyone called the Hoover depression.

Banks closed. Businessmen, unable to comprehend that this was a world-wide depression, urged their customers not to withdraw their money from those banks that remained. My wife and I recognized what was happening and doubtless contributed to the catastrophe, for we withdrew our savings, standing in the long lines that had formed before every teller's window. The next day our bank closed.

Mr. Hearst, who brought high salaries to the newspaper world, did not believe in cutting salaries. He preferred to keep pay up and reduce the staff. I was one of those who kept their jobs. For almost two years Mr. Hearst held the line. No pay cuts. And then suddenly, in rapid succession, came three cuts of ten percent each.

But our household didn't suffer too much. Families were doubling up, or moving to the country and small towns, leaving apartments vacant. Overnight our rent was cut from $85 a month to $50.

Once-wealthy fathers were committing suicide or entering mental homes. Men who had given expensive automobiles to their daughters for college graduation presents were reluctantly taking them back and selling them to anyone with enough money to make any kind of an offer. Breadlines were established to feed the hungry. Long lines of families suddenly on the relief rolls stood in front of groceries, buying the cheapest food they could find.

Advertising fell off, but the newspapers were still the most favored of businesses. Our household was doing so well, before the pay cuts came, that we had moved into Andy Rebori's swank Glass House, a building of duplex apartments with walls of translucent brick.

The Federal Theater was formed, to give work to jobless entertainers, and the government hired my wife as a dance director. The jobless got only a subsistence wage, and we cringed at our own affluence when we had them in for free meals.

Without a doubt, the grimmest experience of my life was the *Her-Ex*'s Great Depression purge, eight hours of horror when one of the most gifted newspaper staffs ever assembled was cut in two because Mr. Hearst still was clinging to his theory that it was better to fire a man than cut his pay. The pay cuts had not yet come. All night, city editor Harry Canfield was calling those who must be let go into his office to give them the bad news and a handshake which he truly meant.

123

The Depression was then at its worst. Firing a man was only slightly less brutal than condemning him to the firing squad. Yet not a member of that staff asked for mercy. There was no word of sick wives and hungry children. No one protested when the ax fell. Night city editor Mike Kennedy told rewriter Delos Avery, "I'll bet you twenty dollars I'm fired." Minutes later, Kennedy was called into Canfield's office. The night city editor came back paler, but still smiling. "I'll take that twenty now," he said. "I've won the bet." And out into the cold he strode, because he had been earning too much money. The highest paid were the first to go, which explains why I stayed on the job.

Kennedy's story was the only happy one of the purge. The more affluent *Tribune* snapped him up immediately and eventually made him Sunday editor. We who were left felt as if we had lived through such an earthquake as comes, sometimes, in dreams. The office seemed a chilly place for months, so chilly that a number of us brought down sweaters to wear under our coats at work. Fred Eldridge had always said Chicago was the goddamnedest town he had ever known for night-breaking news, but now it seemed that the city's tempo had slowed in deference to our lack of manpower to get the news covered. Instead of finding ourselves short-handed, we found that there was not enough work for months on end to keep us busy. We had felt that we were the fortunate ones, to have been spared, but sometimes we wondered when we heard of men we had worked beside still searching hopelessly for jobs. We ducked around corners when we caught sight of them. Rather wryly, now, Canfield repeated the old Romy admonition, "Don't congregate in groups." Its redundancy no longer got a smile. We were too much afraid the front office might see us chatting when we should have been working, and decide to cut the staff even more.

We searched the wire copy for hopeful stories, which by Mr. Hearst's orders we printed under the heading "Good News of Good Times," and we plugged relentlessly the slogan "Prosperity Is Just Around the Corner." But we knew that shivering men were sleeping beneath the Michigan Avenue bridge at night and peddling apples and pencils by day.

When President Franklin D. Roosevelt came in, he tried every kind of pump priming in a vain effort to end the Depression. His Works Progress Administration set the jobless to raking leaves and doing other made work. Unemployed writers were put on the government payroll to produce histories of cities. Artists were employed by the government to paint lugubrious murals in post offices. We hailed the projects as remedies for the nation's ills, but we knew better. It took World War II to end the Depression.

The Depression never touched me, except through the suffering of my friends, a fact that was impressed upon me by the corner newsstand man. I normally left for work at two in the afternoon, but suddenly my hours were changed so that I was due at the office at ten in the morning. The first day that I left our elegant two-story apartment at the new hour, he slapped me heartily on the back and exclaimed, "Getting out in the morning! Mr. Moore, you've found a job."

In all the thirteen years that I worked for the *Her-Ex,* I never saw one member of the Hearst family in the building. Mr. Hearst may have been there on some of his occasional trips between New York and San Simeon, but the absentee owner did not trouble to show himself in the flesh to his minions. Sometimes we heard that his private railroad car was being transferred from one railroad to another in Chicago, and then we all began sharpening our pencils to compute the cost (it was something equivalent to one hundred first-class fares, as office legend had it), so that we might marvel at Mr. Hearst's wealth.

The only time I ever saw him was the afternoon I trudged to Soldiers' Field to hear him take potshots at France for bouncing him out of the Land of the Lilies. It was my day off, but I went out of loyalty and because I feared there might be some subtle way a checkup could be made to determine if any of the staff members had ducked the spectacle when they might have gone. The great man of the *Her-Ex* song "Praise Hearst from Whom All Blessings Flow" had a loud and vibrant voice even in an outdoor stadium that could seat a hundred thousand, but didn't that day. If he had a small audience, it was not the fault of the political editors. They had blackjacked numerous organizations into attending.

Great sections of the stands stood empty. Photographers for rival papers took pictures of them to run with sarcastic captions about the throng that gathered to hear the publisher speak.

Even though we smartcracked about Mr. Hearst and Marion Davies, the rank and file of the *Her-Ex* had a strange affection for him. He might not be perturbed by the empty stands, but we were. We hated with sullen resentment the yes-men who advised him badly, who would not tell him what a man so far removed from the truth about his own organization could not know: that nobody gave a damn about his being expelled from France. Wrong he may often have been; the things his enemies said about him were sometimes true. But editors with the backbone to tell him not to write his often childish Page One editorials and to explain the hypocrisy of some of those who called themselves his friends could have spared him and his papers much.

Mr. Hearst was a terrifying figure and a somewhat supernatural one to the staff. He might close the paper down or, with one of his dread lightning bolts, end the career of a copyreader who had written a headline that had met with the divine disfavor. But he was the Great White Father, kindly as well as just.

Let no one ever think that Mr. Hearst was hated by those who worked for him. We all believed that the *Her-Ex* lost money and that he kept it alive from vanity, a desire to have two papers in Chicago, and a laudable paternalism for his employees.

True, the *Her-Ex* ever reserved the right to fire its men on the spot. We had no group insurance, no formal understanding about sick benefits, no pension plan. The paper wanted us when we were young and enthusiastic and at the top of our game. But we understood that. And it paid us well. We sacrificed job security and written promises of other benefits for money. The *Her-Ex* was a sharp dealer, but we were sharp dealers too. We got more money by threatening to go to other papers.

Yet the sick seldom wanted. Many were the stories of employees Mr. Hearst kept on the payroll through years and years of sickness, and they were not all deserving employees, either. Some of them were drunks, whose illness was a direct result of drinking. We knew, too, and worked with, men who had drunk themselves into uselessness without becoming ill. Like the sick, they were kept on the payroll if they had really given the Great White Father long and brilliant service. He didn't have so much feeling for the plodding kind, but they usually didn't last long on the *Her-Ex* anyway. What you needed there was brilliance, even though you might be half mad.

Even when we were fired, there was always Mr. Hearst. We scarcely felt that we should have to make the appeal, for a good newspaperman could always get another job, before the Depression. But there were many obscure reporters and copyreaders who had saved themselves from destruction by a wrathful managing editor with a telegram to San Simeon. There was, of course, this worry: would the telegram actually reach him? Yet somehow, we felt that it would.

Our belief in a real flesh-and-blood Mr. Hearst was supported by the messages that sometimes came crackling through the space that separated him from us worldlings, asking who had written a particularly sprightly story or headline. Then we knew that the legend that he read every line of every one of his papers must be true, and we waited breathlessly for the compliment that would follow.

Mr. Hearst's representative on earth was Joe Willicombe. He transmitted messages with the awesome introduction "The Chief orders . . ." The Willicombe messages shook the telegraph wires, rattled the building, jarred or elated the staff. They launched "Buy American" campaigns, dictated foreign policy, abolished crime, forbade us to accept decorations from foreign governments, and told us to run direct quotations in blackface type. They began shake-ups, too.

The shake-up was the catastrophe that kept us as worried as anything could keep the staff of such a happy-go-lucky paper worried. It was harder for a dozen men to find new jobs than it was for one. The shake-up was generally in the form of an order to lop $1,000 to $2,000 off the weekly editorial department payroll. That meant firing men, for the *Her-Ex* never cut salaries before the third year of the Depression altered time-tested policies. Shake-ups came most often without warning, but sometimes the New York offices let us know in advance by sending in a crew of efficiency experts, or we heard that the wrecking crew had been in San Francisco or Boston.

The editors always looked grave after a visit by the wrecking crew, for men hired to find inefficiency had to ferret it out. The business and mechanical departments being standardized as they were, the experts had to look for inefficiency in the editorial department, an unorthodox and hideous institution on any newspaper from the businessman's point of view. Since they were unable to understand it, and it was customary any-way, the experts shut one eye and ordered a flat sum, equivalent to the one they had been instructed to save, lopped from its budget.

Sometimes a shake-up meant the dismissal of a publisher, or a managing editor, or a city editor. If there were a place for the man removed, he would be transferred to another paper in the chain, usually at lesser rank and pay. James Bickett, for instance, was deposed after many years of success in building the Chicago *American* as its managing editor and, in his declining years, brought in to serve out his contract as flunky to managing editor Victor Watson. There Bickett was forced to attend to the endless detail heaped upon the shoulders of a day city editor and submit to daily browbeating by everybody from Watson down.

If there was no place for the man who was to be removed,

his contract would be bought and he would be sent into the streets to hunt another job. Forty-thousand-dollar-a-year executives were never free from the specter of unemployment. And when they were swept out, their political henchmen in the organization usually were swept out with them.

If the new managing editor came from New York or any of the other Hearst capitals, he would doubtless bring along a few of his favorites to replace the veterans. If he were a reserve managing editor, who had been lurking in some cubbyhole hopefully waiting for the occasion, he would remove all his predecessor's lieutenants and replace them with followers of his own.

CHAPTER 14

The speakeasies of the era were the playground of the *Her-Ex,* in the days when drinking was fun. Upstairs, downstairs, and on the street they flourished. Nobody ever was turned away, but we got a kick out of pressing the buzzer that alerted a guard who gazed at us through a peephole in the door and then invariably admitted us. In some speaks, part of the ritual was to tell the man at the peephole, "Joe sent me."

There was a thrill in the knowledge that the place might be raided while we were there. But the minions of the law showed up only under the prodding of one of the liquor gangs that was angered at being replaced as the wholesale supplier of gin or the speakeasy owner's refusal to switch his business.

Scotch and bourbon were available at fantastically high prices, but we all drank gin bucks, fashioned from the gin that every gang in town distilled. Whisky was a take-home drink for the family, and we got it not from the speak but from one of the *Her-Ex* reporters who covered the federal building, where

Prohibition enforcement headquarters was. He got it free from stocks confiscated by federal raiders.

Bourbon in bottles that looked legitimate sold for $6 a pint. Scotch was from $8 to $10 a fifth. Gin, in bottles labeled Gordon's, could be bought as low as $5 a fifth, but gin was so easy to make that it was always suspect. Even householders were busy making gin in their bathtubs with juniper berries and all the other ingredients of the celebrated English beverage. Beer in properly labeled bottles was $1.25. If sold from the draft barrels of the Capones, it was 60 cents a glass. All the officials in town knew where the principal Capone brewery was, but nobody did anything about it. Everyone was too thirsty.

Many a man died from drinking bad liquor that contained wood alcohol or something worse. But it wasn't the liquor peddled by the syndicates or the established neighborhood bootlegger. That liquor, genuine or artificially concocted, was safe. The illicit dealers saw to that. Those who died had bought their beverages from amateurs who didn't know the rules, or had stumbled upon some moonshine from the South.

Directly across the street from the paper was the highest-priced speak, which listed itself as a restaurant and did indeed serve fabulous meals to lure the customers in. Diagonally across was the one we frequented most, while in a cellar half a block away was a speak that looked like an old-fashioned saloon, with sawdust on the floor and nudes on the wall.

The speak that called itself Number Seven was the favorite of editors and staff members who worked until the small hours, because of Blackie. He was a runty little man who seldom spoke. But he performed a valuable service for the late-stayers, driving them home in his ancient car. For a dollar, he would deliver them anyplace within the city, for two dollars to any North Shore suburb. One hard-drinking editor was a nightly rider in the winter months. He had a phobia that if he took a suburban train he might fall down in the snow on his one-block walk home from the station and freeze to death.

Tom Michelmore, for a time the night city editor, preferred

an upstairs speak where the pork chops were luscious. At one in the morning he would insist that I go with him. After half a dozen beers he would order a pork chop sandwich. Virtuously explaining that he was trying to keep down his weight, he would throw away the bread, eat the chop, and then down half a dozen more beers.

A block and a half away was an elegant Italian speak, where the horse that threw and killed gangster chief Nails Morton was ordered executed. Nails had lately gone high hat and, when things in the gang he ruled weren't too pressing, had taken to riding in the park in a bright red horseman's coat. Never having been properly trained to ride, he fell on his head when his mount shied and was killed.

Nails's stout-hearted henchmen gathered at the Italian speak long after midnight on the day of the funeral and held court, with a prosecutor and a defense attorney. The defendant was the horse, and the charge was murder. His lawyer made a vigorous defense, but the jury of gangsters found him guilty and decreed the death penalty. Next day the gang took the horse to the forest preserve and shot him. Nails Morton was avenged.

Great ideas were evolved in the speaks. For instance, naming the area that was the home of Mr. Hearst's *Her-Ex* and *American,* Hearst Square. The area was also the home of the Chicago *Daily News.* The area had no name, but, because the *Her-Ex* was known as the Madhouse of Madison Street, it was sometimes described by gagsters as Madhouse Square.

And then a flash of genius came to a brilliant reporter in an upstairs speak: Name it Hearst Square. His drinking companions spread the word, and soon there was an all-out campaign to establish the name, whether the *Daily News* liked it or not. For years, *Her-Ex* officials covertly used their influence in an eventually unsuccessful effort to establish Hearst Square, with the *Daily News* as an unwilling captive of the compound.

The end of thirteen years of Prohibition in 1933 was truly the end of an era. There were no longer any giant liquor gangs to make front-page news with their bloody wars. They shrank back to their pre-Prohibition size and returned to their old rackets of gambling and prostitution. The speaks that had flourished in stately old mansions turned into respectable restaurants. The upstairs and cellar dives went out of business.

Misguided members of the Bugs Moran gang, convinced that the dark and comfortable barrooms of the old days were passé in a modern age, set up their idea of what a saloon should be around the corner from the *Her-Ex.* It was brightly lighted and looked like a cafeteria. Instead of pig's knuckles and sauerkraut, there was a sumptuous buffet, tables and tables of free lunch. Reporters of the three newspapers of the neighborhood came in, ordered a martini, and ate a couple of dollars' worth of free food.

All the bums on Madison Street's nearby Skid Row took their meals there, without buying the martini. The place lasted three weeks, and the gangsters fled to Cicero, long-time stronghold of gangland, to make an honest living off the earnings of prostitutes.

The old Scrooge Fred Eldridge, whom we called both Dracula and the Smiling Lieutenant, was, unbeknownst to me, the greatest friend I ever had on the paper. He never gave me a pleasant smile, but it was he who brought me back to the *Her-Ex* after I had been fired.

When I was severed, I had found myself a job at the City News Bureau, better known as the City Press, a news-gathering agency maintained by all the Chicago dailies to supplement their own news coverage. The City Press covered all the news and sent its stories by underground tube to the papers. Much of what it covered was routine, but it frequently turned up stories that might otherwise have been overlooked, and if there was not enough the papers rewrote them or assigned their own reporters to follow them up.

The City Press was a training school whose successful alumni progressed to better jobs on the papers. The organization was therefore reversing policy in hiring me, since I had already worked on the *Her-Ex* and was not ordinarily eligible for employment. There was a vacancy, however, left by the reporter who covered the hotel beat when he landed a job on the *Daily News*, and editor Emil Hubka hired me as a replacement.

One day a friendly room clerk at the Congress Hotel told me that Pat Harrison was a guest, and I arranged to interview him.

Pat was riding high then, as senior senator from Mississippi and a raconteur who never failed to delight the guests at the gay Washington parties given by Alice Roosevelt Longworth, Dolly Gann, and other contemporary hostesses.

Pat received me in his suite wearing long underwear and nothing else, although it was a hot day, and proceeded to regale me with a story of Vice President Charlie Dawes's falling asleep while presiding over the Senate.

The *Her-Ex* ran my story as I wrote it, and, since it was a City Press story, there was no by-line. But it was on Page One, and soon afterward I was rehired.

Long years afterward Jack Malloy was cleaning out his desk when he came upon a note written by Fred Eldridge, supervising managing editor. I doubt that he even knew me personally then, but he had investigated the authorship of the story and scribbled this note to the city desk:

"Great story, Pat Harrison in his underwear. Understand this man has been fired. Get him back."

On another occasion, I got Eldridge's boost in advance. After the three *Her-Ex* Depression pay cuts I had found myself that rarity of the Depression, another job at higher pay. I hadn't told anyone, but somehow the word got to Eldridge while I was still considering whether to make a move or not.

After the first edition had gone to press one day, Jack McPhaul, then day city editor, asked me if I would go through his personal papers on his desk spindle and throw out everything that wasn't important. Halfway down I discovered what he wanted me to find, again a note from Eldridge.

"Understand this man Moore has been offered a better job," it read. "He's great. Match any offer he gets."

I promptly submitted my resignation and named my price for staying—all three of my pay cuts back. I got them courtesy of Dracula.

Newspaper people are a fascinating lot. McPhaul sat on the city desk for years before he found out why the Shuberts were so free with their passes. He had a friend who worked for them, and the friend had invited him to ask for passes any time he wished to see a show in a Shubert theater. Old ethical Jack wouldn't ask the management, but did eventually agree to let his friend know, at home, when he needed tickets. Whenever he wanted to see a Shubert show thereafter, McPhaul would communicate his desire to his friend. That night, tickets would be waiting for him at the box office.

After years of theater-going on his friend's passes, McPhaul chanced to ask his friend how the Shuberts were doing. "I don't know," his friend told him. "I haven't been with them for years."

"Then how," inquired the astounded Mr. McPhaul, "have you been getting me all those ducats?" "Oh, that," his friend replied. "That's nothing at all. I've always just called the Shubert office, said I was Jack McPhaul of the *Herald & Examiner,* and told them to put two tickets away for me. Why don't you try calling them yourself sometime? They're happy to do it, for a newspaper."

Mr. McPhaul was shocked out of his shoes. From that time on he bought his tickets at the box office, personally.

Sam Blair, one of the *Her-Ex* greats who had an uncanny nose for finding the right lilac bush under which to dig for the husband the kindly old grandmother had bumped off and buried in the front lawn, had trouble one summer with a neurotic neighbor. It was the neighbor's annoying habit to keep watch on the Blair apartment and hammer on the door with a baseball bat when he thought the family was making too much noise, at any time of the day or night. Without a doubt the most thorough gentleman I have ever known on a newspaper, courtly Mr. Blair shuddered at getting the fellow into trouble. But, since something had to be done, he got a bat of his own. He chased his annoyer away a few times, and, finding that did no good, counseled with the police reporters on what to do with him.

They knew precisely what to do. Police reporters always do when it's your trouble. If you do what they tell you to, and it works, they try it themselves. In this case, they advised Mr. Blair to explain his troubles to a friendly judge, whom they would choose. The judge would send the annoyer off to the mental hospital, paving the way for relief if the man were really mentally deficient, or instilling a little fear in him if he were merely annoying. Mr. Blair chuckled. He invited Mrs. Blair to come along for a laugh. But, before the hearing had begun, he was called away on a story.

Confident that all arrangements had been made, he left Mrs. Blair to attend to the details. The judge heard the case, ordered the fellow to the hospital as scheduled, and sent Mrs. Blair along to explain. But his Honor, an absent-minded if accommodating jurist, neglected to give his bailiff a fill-in. When the sheriff's car reached the hospital, the attendants took both the annoying neighbor and Mrs. Blair in tow. She smiled in the confidence that the authorities were putting on a show to convince the annoying neighbor and any friends he might have that no favoritism was being shown.

But her smile left her face when they began giving her a mental examination. In vain did she explain when they handed her the building blocks for her first test. Although she was a newspaperwoman herself, and a brilliant one, this was something for which she was scarcely prepared. The neighbor put his blocks together, answered most of the questions correctly, and was on his way in half an hour. Mrs. Blair, looking for a trap that wasn't there in every test, was hours getting out. And then the psychiatrist told her to return on the next day, just to be sure.

One of the major kidnappings of Chicago's history was that of Billy Ranieri. I was sitting beside the city desk when word came that Billy had been released at Lockport, Illinois. Thomas Barry, a fine newspaperman who was later a publisher on the West Coast, was chatting with Harry Canfield, the night city editor.

"My car's outside," said Barry. "It's a new one that will do ninety. Give me a photographer and let me go."

"Go, and God be with you," said Canfield cynically.

An hour passed. No word from Tom. An hour and a half, ample time to get there, the way he drove. No word. Two hours and ten minutes. Then came Tom's call.

"I'm in Rockford, all right," reported the man who should have been in Lockport. "But nobody here knows anything about Billy Ranieri."

Canfield knew that he was scooped, and badly. He had missed a first-hand account of the kidnapping from the kidnapped boy. Worse, he had missed the pictures, which he knew would fill the back page of the opposition. But the toughest editor in the racket, and one of the squarest shooting, rolled on the city desk in laughter.

"Never say a word about this to either of them," he said when he was able to speak again. "They're going through enough hell now to last them the rest of their lives."

The staff watched with interest the night that one of the rewriters decided, after an extra drink, that the city room was home. With fitting modesty he pulled down the window shade nearest his desk. Then, while girl reporters streaked from the side door, he solemnly undressed. He hung his coat and shirt over the back of his chair and placed his trousers, neatly folded, on the floor. Removing his shorts, he snapped off his desk light, raised the shade again, opened the window, said,

"Goodnight, Patricia," and lay down to slumber beside his trousers on the floor.

All the zanies weren't on our paper. I discovered this when I was sent up to St. Joseph, Michigan, to cover a murder trial. A beautiful blonde had shot and killed her sweetie, the sheriff. Bob Casey, then Chicago's favorite author and the star reporter on the *Daily News,* was also assigned. I never saw him in the courtroom, nor did any legman appear for him at the press table. Yet the *Daily News* published a story of the trial under his by-line every day, and the stories were masterpieces of accuracy.

The trial taught me one thing: Never be photographed with a drink in your hand. The House of David, a long-haired, bearded, religious cult, had its farm in the vicinity. Although it recruited baseball players, equipped them with beards and shoulder-length hair, and sent them out to play semi-pro ball, the House hadn't hit the front pages since the turbulent days of its King Benjamin, two decades earlier. The current head of the religious colony was a man who had achieved success as a lawyer before taking over the colony's rich farmlands. He volunteered to represent the comely defendant.

The House had some strict rules, among them a ban on eating meat, but it had a plush nightclub, which served not meat but synthetic steaks. The liquor flowed freely, for that was not among the things the faithful shunned.

As the trial drew near its end, the lawyer and religious leader closed the nightclub for the night for a party honoring the press. I was standing there with a martini in my hand when a photographer for a local paper approached. He wanted a picture of me with the religious leaders, long hair, hairpins, and all. I tried to duck, but everyone assured me the pictures would be as private as the party: mementos for our families. I posed, with the leaders' arms around me.

The following morning I got a telephone call from my publisher. "You were sent up there to cover a story," he said indignantly. "What are you doing carousing with a lot of long-hairs?"

My paper came in. The picture was on the back page.

Crime reporter Austin O'Malley of the *Her-Ex* had been laboring for years on a dictionary of underworld slang, when he bumped into a confidence man known as Sixth Avenue Benson. Sixth Avenue was broke, and they made a deal: O'Malley would keep Sixth Avenue in cakes, since Sixth Avenue was too hot to risk being put under glass by earning an honest living selling the Grant statue or the Hotel Sherman, as confidence men were doing then. (They even supplied the sucker with a key guaranteed to lock or unlock the hotel, when they were peddling it.) Sixth Avenue, in turn, would talk to O'Malley in prison language.

Because several other underworld slang dictionaries were being written, O'Malley felt it was essential to keep his plans secret; in particular, he wished to keep Sixth Avenue under cover.

But Sixth Avenue made the acquaintance of a Northwestern University professor who invited him to the campus to address the students in prison jargon. Sixth Avenue's colorful terminology got him into the papers, under an assumed name. He was promptly invited to speak at the University of Chicago. Within a week he was the darling of the educators, spilling all his own choice information, and O'Malley's, in lectures that went into the papers where his linguistic morsels could be read by O'Malley's competitors. Once Sixth Avenue had tasted publicity, through which he was protected from the law, he never had time to sit around dishing out crime slang for O'Malley any more. One listener, when he might have a thousand? Preposterous, and a lot of other adjectives the professors had taught him. As O'Malley put it, Sixth Avenue thereafter drove past him on an ice wagon.

Phi Beta Kappas know a lot of abstruse things, but some of them don't know what any farm boy knows, that steers don't beget progeny. I found that out when I was assigned to head a staff to cover the International Live Stock Show. My staff was one man, a proud wearer of the Phi Beta Kappa key, and I was happy to have so erudite a gentleman aboard.

Just to be safe, I read copy on his stories until the night the grand champion was chosen. My eager beaver, now a wheel on a Chicago paper, went out to interview the young owner, whose hayseed friends decided to take in the city slicker reporter. That time I neglected to read his story. It began, "The grand champion steer was chosen last night at the International Live Stock Show. He is a grandson of the grand champion of three years ago."

Slats Slattery, one of the best rewrite men the *Her-Ex* ever produced, was a true eccentric. Walter Howey, featured in *The Front Page* as Walter Burns, once offended Slats by refusing to raise his pay to $175 a week. It wasn't the money, with Slats. It was the principle. Other top rewrite men were getting $150, and he wanted it clearly established that he was the top banana. When he was refused, he retired to his home in a huff, announcing as he slammed the office door behind him that he would henceforth devote his life to raising a beard.

No mollycoddle, Howey held out for three days, refusing to recognize his ace's absence. Then he began to worry. Slats was really staying at home and raising a beard. Howey's worries turned to nightmares of Slats in a long white beaver who would never be around at deadline time. The managing editor began telephoning an appeal several times a day, but Slats was adamant; he was going to raise a beard and do nothing else. Howey went to visit him, threatened him, beseeched him, but Slats, in unshaven dignity, refused to budge for even a bigger raise than he had asked. At last, in desperation, Howey gave him more money than Slats had ever dreamed of getting and threw in a humble apology. Solemnly, but triumphantly, Slats returned to work.

CHAPTER 15

Prohibition was unpopular, and drinking was becoming a national pastime. Franklin D. Roosevelt was only one of the nation's top figures who opposed Prohibition. Mabel Walker Willebrandt, an assistant United States attorney general, retired and went to work as counsel for an organization that sold fruit bricks from which wine could be made. Soon she was hailed as the nation's leading woman lawyer.

When public officials charged with suppressing bootlegging were running for re-election and were under the fire of better-government organizations, they simply had their homes bombed (harmlessly, of course) to demonstrate that they were the victims, rather than the allies, of gangland.

Through it all, the *Her-Ex* maintained a position of unadulterated nuttiness. A charming paper and an incredible one! A storybook paper that never found out which were the giants and which the windmills. A childlike paper, with its eager little nose pressing against the toy shop window, but its childishness was that of the city kid, for it packed a gat on its hip in case of a circulation war.

If a rival paper sent a relief train to some state struck by a disaster, the *Her-Ex* editors were there. At press time they would send a trusted copyboy to the rival's composing room with a note directing an immediate change in the caption for the picture of the relief train. The note would bear a signature approximating that of the rival's managing editor. And in its final edition, the rival paper would be astonished to find its relief train designated as the *Herald & Examiner*'s.

The owlish wit of the *Her-Ex* editors hit its high when another paper decided to celebrate an anniversary. It laid pompous plans for a civic celebration. But the *Her-Ex* editors called upon the Hearst organization for help. On the appointed day the city was overrun with loudspeaker trucks bearing such notables as Bugs Baer, Damon Runyon, Rube Goldberg, Walter Winchell, and actors portraying everybody from Snuffy Smith to Popeye. It was a *Her-Ex* day.

We were great on promotions. Through advertising schemes, public service, battles for the underdog, and pure luck, we kept our relationship with our readers pleasant, if not in some cases actually deliriously happy. Promotion was an art at the *Her-Ex;* if not a fine art, it was at least one that paid magnificent returns, in circulation, revenue, and goodwill.

The promotion manager, Emil Garber, sometimes gave away yo-yos. Sometimes he published best sellers serially. Yo-yos, comeback balls, a hundred and one games played with balls attached to paddles by an elastic cord, and miniature pool tables seemed to be the most consistent circulation getters. Sometimes there were free dictionaries or baseball gloves to be had with subscriptions. Occasionally the inducement was an insurance policy or a coaster wagon.

The paper promoted cooking schools at which prizes were awarded without the expenditure of a dime. The advertisers paid the bills. Stage stars and the great orchestras of the day furnished the entertainment, for nix. The only entertainer I knew to object to the sand-bagging was Joe Cook, and he got there on time all right, wearing his happiest smile, after being asked, "What the hell, Joe?"

It was a dull week when there wasn't a contest running in the *Her-Ex*. Colossal ones with large prizes were impressive, but the editors complained that too often these were won by readers with unpronounceable names who lived in the sticks, and the advertising department beefed that that sort of thing helped little in building up the legend that *Her-Ex* circulation was concentrated in the metropolitan district, where the buyers were.

For that reason, smaller contests were popular with the masterminds, since the winners and their addresses in the sticks need not be listed on Page One. There were fantastic contests. Borrowing a page from Hermann Rorschach, the Swiss psychiatrist, we gave our readers authentic Rorschach tests, urging them to shake a drop of ink from their pens upon a piece of paper and fold the paper in the middle to make a blot. Naturally, we couldn't interpret the test, but sometimes the blot would look like a butterfly when it dried, or Harpo Marx, or a superannuated aardvark, and, if the rewrite man sitting in as contest editor for the day liked it, it might win a $2 prize. One winner made it with Noah's Ark. Half the readers divided their time between flipping ink from pens and trying to win a yo-yo. This, younger readers, was before the ballpoint pen, when fountain pens had ink in them.

It was fascinating entertainment the *Her-Ex* provided. When Knock-Knock came along, the paper gave its name its blessing, and made it a household game. Readers were invited to send in pet peeves, the most peevish of which won prizes dealt out with a lavish hand, if not too careful a one, by the reporter or rewriter who happened to be the current contest judge. Motorboat races, model airplane contests, and competitions to choose the city's best ballroom dancers kept the paper busy.

But it was the reporters who made the paper. When Queen

Marie of Rumania came to town, and the Four Hundred decreed that the party in her honor should be strictly private, half a dozen newsmen got jobs as waiters and waitresses and reported everything she said.

When Judge Kenesaw Mountain Landis outlawed Shoeless Joe Jackson and his colleagues in the Chicago White Sox baseball scandal in 1919, it was *Her-Ex* reporter Alan Hathaway who was cozying up to the federal judge's secretary and reading the finding as she typed it, for a scoop, over her shoulder.

I never had heard of colored toilet paper until Jane Eads came in from a gangster's love nest after he had been assassinated. She had a roll of it—lavender. It was just out. Jane's romance with Seymour Berkson, whom she eventually married, was a classic of the *Her-Ex*. When they quarreled, one of them would patch things up by laying an apple on the other's desk.

One of my favorites was Pat Peabody of the coal mine family. He flew his own airplane from his home in a fashionable North Shore suburb, to work for $35 a week and the prestige of a place on the *Her-Ex* staff. Good old Pat never has paid me the $5 he borrowed one day to buy gas for his plane.

Pat had been a precocious lad with a youthful love for banned books. Around the corner from the Drake Hotel was his favorite bookstore. But he couldn't buy the books he wanted. He had, however, a young governess with whom, his friends said, he was having a romance. And so they would drive up in a Packard and she would get him the books he craved. She looked to be over twenty-one. That was progress for a boy of fourteen.

The only *Her-Ex* reporter I ever encountered who knew where he was going was Jonathan (Jack) Latimer, best known later as a scenarist for the "Perry Mason" television show. He was a sensitive and well-educated young man who joined the *Her-Ex* for its glamor and found himself getting lousy assignments. One time he returned from a dismal tour of a coal mine disaster area and told me he was going to Hollywood. "I have connections," he said, "and I can get by if I can write." He departed and became one of the movie industry's foremost writing stars.

The besetting sin of the wandering reporters who found jobs at the *Her-Ex* was their letter writing. No sooner would one of them turn in a good story than in would come dozens of letters, ostensibly from happy readers, praising the story and the man who wrote it. Having become accustomed to this sort of thing over a long period of years, the city editor always investigated the persons whose names were signed. Invariably he found them nonexistent. One reporter was assigned to go to Nicaragua with the Marines. He asked all his kinfolk to write letters of adulation for his stories. The assignment was called off, but the letters poured in.

Can you imagine close friends coming up to you and saying, "Hello, Baboon Face Moore"? I certainly can't. But go through the list of Chicago's gangsters, and you'll find their nicknames couldn't have been used by most of their compatriots. The truth is that those monikers were hung on the gangsters by the press, and most of them by Romy. Before his death he'd have denied it if you had ascribed any of them to him, but he'd have loved your suggesting it. Some of them were:

Ammunition Eddie, Ashcan Pete, Baby Face Willie Doody, Big Rabbit Connel and his brother Little Rabbit, Bon Bon Allegretti, Chicago May Churchill, Cock-eyed Mulligan, Dynamite Pete, Golf Bag Sammie, Hymie the Slob, Ice Wagon Connors, Jakie the Torch, Jesse the Goof, Louis the Louse, Lovin' Putty, Machine Gun Jack McGurn, Mike de Pike, Monkeyface Charlie, Smiling Sammie Samoots, Paddy the Cub and Paddy the Bear, Scarface Al Capone, and the best gangland name of all, Trouble Tribble. There were Diamond Jim, Diamond Joe, and Diamond Louis, all named for their love of wearing diamonds. Smiling Sammie Samoots was the gunman who taught gangland to carry sawed-off shotguns in violin cases. His enemies murdered him in a barber's chair, where he was getting prettied up to go white-tie to the opera. A movie was made about him and his violin case.

Arthur Meeker of the packing family was a member of our staff when he won acclaim as a novelist. Basil Woon, already established as an author, came aboard briefly. Victor Watson hired him at a fabulous salary to cover the murder trial of the Widow Pollack, who called her husband Poor Joe in respect of how he looked when she shot him. Mindful of the fact that Woon wasn't a newspaperman, Watson sent Carol Frink to back him up. She wrote such sparkling stories, for use if substitute copy were needed, that the editors used hers instead of Woon's, and Woon bowed hastily out.

Johnny Weismuller never worked on the *Her-Ex,* but we all regarded the celebrated swimmer as a member of the family. One afternoon the *Favorite,* an excursion boat, went down with a load of children right off the Chicago beach. Johnny was returning from a swim far out in Lake Michigan. He promptly set about rescuing all the children he could. Eugene McDonald, the head of the Zenith radio corporation, directed operations from his yacht.

CHAPTER 16

ETAOIN SHRDLU.

There it was, right at the end of an editorial conceding that Mayor Big Bill Thompson might have been harshly judged for threatening to punch King George of Great Britain in the snoot.

City editor Duffy Cornell beckoned me. "The mayor just called in a huff," said Duffy. "Says ETAOIN SHRDLU at the end of our editorial means 'Baloney.' Calls it one of our backhand slaps at him. That damned unpronounceable phrase pops up in our paper too often.

"I want you to get me the story on ETAOIN SHRDLU. Take the next train to Baltimore. That's where Ottmar Mergenthaler invented the Linotype machine, and it's the Linotype machine that's doing it."

"But, Boss," I protested, "you've just assigned me to do a series on Piltdown Man."

"Never mind Piltdown Man!" Duffy retorted. "That was the mistake of a San Francisco reporter who fell for the story of a silly old horse doctor. Hearst fired him. You get on ETAOIN SHRDLU."

Many suspected that ETAOIN SHRDLU was an irrepressible gremlin whom Ottmar never was able to get out of the machine that he invented to free the newspapers and book and magazine publishers from the awesome task of typesetting by hand. Obviously of the Democratic persuasion, ETAOIN SHRDLU would follow any compliment to the Republicans, as if to say "Hogwash."

For the first half of this century, ETAOIN SHRDLU was the darling of proofreaders, the despair of editors, and the love of readers who collected newspaper typos. Society writers complained bitterly when ETAOIN showed up to give lie to the comment that the bride was lovely. Even obituaries were not immune to the rollicking phrase.

Proofreaders loved ETAOIN, who popped up every so often to brighten their drab lives. He was always apropos. They wouldn't have thought of deleting him, and if there was a protest from the editors, the blue-pencil wielders retorted that the light in the proofroom was bad.

The Linotype operators themselves had various explanations of the phenomenon. Practical-minded ones tried to explain ETAOIN away as a result of the law of averages. They were bound to make a certain number of mistakes, they said, and the letters they used most often, in their next-to-human machines, would drop them into the type when twelve errors had been made—the precise number of letters in ETAOIN SHRDLU.

These apologists for Ottmar's masterpiece never could prove their theory. It failed to account for the fact that the letter *M,* one of the busiest in the alphabet, never got in. And why were the letters all capitals?

Superstitious old-timers never failed to recite the experience of a jobless member of their craft who made the rounds of the printing shops in San Francisco, wandered into the unlocked door of one that was idle, commandeered a machine, and spent the Sabbath tapping out the letter *a*. He reported that ETAOIN SHRDLU came up at regular intervals in caps, although the letter he tapped was not a capital, but lower case.

In Baltimore I found a story that Etaoin had been a real live human being, a distant relative who helped Ottmar with his invention. Etaoin, as the story went, was a fun-loving fellow who bugged the machine so cleverly that Ottmar never could find out why ETAOIN SHRDLU fell into the type with such surprising regularity.

A more sinister tale, doubtless apocryphal, was that Etaoin secretly bought into a firm that supplied Ottmar with papier-mâché, and bugged the machine in revenge when Ottmar gave up trying to devise a typesetting machine of papier-mâché and brought out the metal Linotype instead.

Great scholars have tried in vain for decades to explain ETAOIN SHRDLU. Einstein is said to have inclined to the belief that the original Linotype was bugged and that the bug had somehow persisted in the complicated mechanism. Houdini is said to have accepted this theory and carried it a step further: that the bug was psychic and could drop ETAOIN in wherever it hurt most.

I have long been one of those who doubt that ETAOIN SHRDLU ever existed as a person. No human being, it seems to me, could have gone through life trying to explain how to pronounce a name spelled like that.

"It has been a long time," I wrote in my memo to Duffy Cornell, "since Ottmar perfected the Linotype in 1885. Memories have dimmed. The Baltimore city directories of that time list no Etaoin Shrdlu."

Duffy's reaction was brief and typical.

"Okay, you fell down on the Baltimore assignment," he said. "And you padded your expense account. What the hell am I going to tell Big Bill? Now get back to Piltdown Man. I get it that he had new glands installed before the society playboys ever heard of it."

Whether he was a man or a bug, ETAOIN SHRDLU's

name is rarely seen in the newspapers these days. One reason may be the long lines of Linotype machines with no operators. The punched tape that has replaced the operators doesn't turn out ETAOINS any more. But that doesn't really explain the mystery.

I learned early in life about libel suits and how to avoid them. The *Her-Ex* morgue saw to that. When we ordered clippings, they were marked in big black letters, "Watch out for libel," if the subject had ever sued for libel or threatened to. The closest I have ever come to getting a paper into a libel suit was a *Her-Ex* series on Dave Barry, the long-count referee of the Dempsey-Tunney fight.

Long after his days as a referee, Barry became involved with some ex-convicts in Chicago. The group took over a small Chicago bank, and presently they were accused of looting it. Barry's defense was that he was a simple country boy who hadn't known what he was getting into. Considering his record of refereeing big-time fights in the big towns, the *Her-Ex* editors regarded this as ridiculous. They told me to write the story of the trial and to hit the country boy story hard. I did. Barry came out looking like a confidence man who dwarfed Yellow Kid Weil, the foremost con man of the first half of the century.

Then the verdict came in. The ex-convicts were found guilty, and Barry was acquitted. He prepared to sue the *Her-Ex* for a million dollars. I sweated. I had no money, so he couldn't collect anything from me, but a million-dollar judgment in his favor would end my career as a reporter. Just as my situation was becoming impossible, Barry died, ending the libel proceedings.

I have always been opposed to capital punishment, and I shall always be, but you don't choose your assignments on a newspaper. When I was told to cover a double electrocution, I covered it. The mayor was there. The sheriff was there. High society—anyone who could get tickets—was there. What the thrill is of seeing a man's life snuffed out is something I have never figured out. To me, the whole performance was one of barbarity, and my principal memory of it was the stench of burning flesh. But I went back to the office and wrote the story in time for the next deadline, because city editor Harry Read had sent reporter Joe Fay out to pick me up.

My next assignment was a pure joy. A lady had cleaned her $2,000 diamond ring and wrapped it in a tissue to dry. Her maid had dropped it down the drain, thinking the whole package was waste. Well, the city sewerage officials set to work. They trapped that diamond, when the experts said the odds were twenty million to one against them.

Turkey Gerke was one of the *Her-Ex* favorites. In the summer and fall he was a simple bartender in Watertown, Wisconsin. In the winter he became a national celebrity. He didn't like the northern winters, and so he just went to bed and hibernated until summer came again.

Back in the 1920s, sea monsters became something of an international vogue. That thing in Loch Ness was always popping up, and it wasn't long until a down-and-out press agent I had known for a long time came in to inquire if I knew anyone who would give a hundred dollars for a sure-fire monster. He had a mechanical one rigged up so that he could direct it by wires from some secluded spot on shore, and he thought some enterprising businessman ought to be glad to have it known that a genuine sea monster was haunting the beach near his place of business. You will understand, then, why I was skeptical when two days later the residents of the South Shore district began reporting a monster that swam in the lake.

The first reports were somewhat vague, but news of the monster sent thousands scurrying to the beach to watch. By the end of the second day, bathers were almost afraid to go into the water, and those who did came back terrified, although still alive, with stories of being chased by the monster. There were a few who insisted that the creature had come up on the land and pursued them.

Then an attendant at the aquarium confessed. He had been

151

ordered to put to death a seal, known to the staff as Oscar, which had developed some seal malaise comparable to tuberculosis in a human being. Unable to bring himself to looking Oscar in the eye and killing him, the tender-hearted attendant put the seal in a tub one night, carried him to the lake, and told him to go and swim some more.

That was all there was to the sea monster story—that and the fact that Oscar eventually died and was cast up on the shore, after he had fattened considerably on the fish that he took from fishermen's lines along the piers. But the entire city talked about that seal for weeks, more than about the Great Depression, which was then raging. The press agent was exonerated.

It was the age of the individual press agent, before the big public relations firms took over. A press agent might have a restaurant as a client, or a theater, or a hotel, or he might have half a dozen accounts. He depended for his livelihood on his friendship with reporters and editors.

Press agentry was developed to its funniest and most uproarious stage during Chicago's Century of Progress Exposition in 1933 and 1934. Sally Rand set the stage by jumping into the lake from a speedboat. It made Page One. Then Ruth Pryor tried it. Before the fair was over, every dancer who could swim had been pulled out of the lake at least once, and some of the better swimmers several times. A whole dancing chorus jumped into the lake one night.

Jumping into the lake, of course, was only a minor episode in the life of Sally Rand, who had already established herself as a national figure by convincing the country, and the courts, that a lady need not wear pants.

Of all the World's Fair press agents, William Harshe displayed the greatest imagination. It was he who thought of the sparkling idea of shoes for an elephant. Every paper in town carried pictures of the elephant that Harshe had shod, because, he said innocently, its feet were tender. And it was he who contrived the escape of the first of the monkeys which, so far as could be ascertained, traveled by the Illinois Central electric lines to the Jackson Park yacht harbor, each monkey on a different day, boarded a ship, and calculatingly bit the ship's captain.

Chuck Dural put the tightrope walker Bunny Dryden on the great cable of the Sky Ride, and realized when it was too late to stop him that he probably was sending the poor fellow to his death. For years, it seemed to Duval, Dryden balanced on that cable in the wind that had suddenly come up and, eventually, to the wonderment of everyone, got safely across from the east tower to the west.

The fair's press agents used the courts shamelessly. If they could get the entertainers in their shows arrested, particularly for nudity, gate receipts were certain to increase, for an otherwise apathetic public would travel far to see Venus on the Half Shell or the Black Panther Woman if they had been arrested and sentenced to jail. The sketch classes at the Streets of Paris never became popular, for all their nudity, until press agent Cati Mount was able to get one of the models on the police blotter. (Odd name that, isn't it? Press agents seem to be born with them. One of the best, who used to handle Texas Guinan, called himself Rasputin. Not Mr. Rasputin. Just Rasputin.)

It was the press agents who made the tawdry section of North Clark Street Chicago's real night-life center during the fair. A nightclub of the district, whose entrance was marked by an ancient hansom cab, chanced to get a particularly alert press agent, Lew Fink. He loaded himself and a dozen plump chorus girls from one of those ballets known as a beef trust troupe into the cab and set out for the Loop. As he had loosened the wheels by way of extra precaution, the venerable hansom, like the one-hoss shay, folded up. Fell to pieces. The press agent hurried into court with a lawyer hired by his employer and filed a damage suit against his employer, in the name of the girls. It made Page One.

Fink was no believer in class distinction. While he represented the Clark Street joint, he also did public relations work for a swank Oak Street restaurant, almost across the street from the plush Drake Hotel. The big moment was the Thanksgiving season. Then he placed an enormous turkey in a cage in the front window. The turkey was close enough to touch the diners as they came and went. And one of those who came and went was always a beautiful blonde in Fink's employ. She stopped to observe the turkey and wham! She and the restaurant were on Page One, for she brought suit charging that the turkey plucked the $5,000 diamond out of her ring and gobbled it. Fink earned his money.

Other press agents caught the World's Fair spirit. There was the church press agent who sent in an up-to-the-minute advance obituary every day during the long and eventually fatal illness of his bishop. If a press agent of mine ever predicted my death to the newspapers every day, I should make a point of getting well for the express purpose of firing him.

There was the press agent for the girl evangelist who was seventeen for so many years. That agent, a woman, bombarded our office for one whole evening with telephone announcements that the girl soul-saver had just been arrested in the Loop while delivering a sermon. Investigation brought information that the girl evangelist had spent the night jumping up on a soap box in assorted sections of the Loop and that each time a policeman, who couldn't possibly have cared unless he were being paid for it, had bobbed up to tell her she was under arrest, although no one was exactly clear as to what the charge was. Never once was she hauled off to the station.

There was the agent who obligingly interrupted one of Aimee Semple McPherson's religious services for me, so that our photographer might get a picture of her and her daughter kneeling before a cross. I shall never forget that her daughter's fingernails were dirty.

Some sharpies were their own press agents. H. Bedford

Jones was in town for a court trial—his own. Jones, who made a fortune writing adventure stories for the pulp magazines, held a seminar for newspaper folk who wanted to write for the pulps. He made the headlines with his story that he never had the money in his early days to travel to the countries he wrote about. When he'd made his millions, he confessed, he traveled to them and found them exactly like he had thought they'd be. His seminar was a bust. He hadn't the foggiest idea of what to tell us about why he was a success. But there he was, a self-made millionaire, and there were we, the press, working for peanuts.

In an age when there wasn't any Vietnam war, and nobody gave a hang about foreign relations, I had Chicagoans weeping or laughing with stories that couldn't get into the papers these days. For instance:

TEN THOUSAND MILES

Ten thousand miles, all the way to the ice floes of Little America.

Francis Black's voice doesn't break. Sons of men with the Byrd expedition don't cry. Not when they're four years old. Francis Black is very calm when he steps up there and says:

"Hello, Daddy!"

It's the crowd in the Columbia Broadcasting System studio in the Wrigley building that's choking back the tears. For all his tragic loneliness, they aren't thinking about the boy so much as his father. Richard Black knows what they haven't told his son yet—that the boy's mother is dead. Francis's aged grandparents have told him she went to Little America to be with his father.

Even the son of a man with the expedition can't deny that he's lonely.

"I sure miss you. I'll be waiting for you, Daddy, and

I hope you'll be back soon. And don't forget to bring me that husky you promised."

Then from that ice floe, ten thousand miles away: "Hello, Fran. I hear you. And I'll bring you the husky pup. It's to be from Admiral Byrd himself. He told me last night he'd have it for you. Goodnight, Boy."

That brown-eyed boy from Grand Forks, South Dakota, doesn't care if the rest of the world is listening in on the regular Wednesday night broadcast. He shouts, just as if no one else can hear:

"Goodnight, Daddy. I love you!"

THE CANNIBALS

Terribly misunderstood fellows, cannibals. The last thing they'd do, that you'd ever hear about, is eat you, and then not if you'd been properly introduced. They don't even like being cannibals.

The ones in New Guinea, anyway, eat only their enemies, and they really wouldn't eat them, except to show that they're not becoming sentimental.

Dr. Margaret Mead of the American Museum of Natural History, who is lecturing at the University of Chicago on life among the cannibals, explained it last night at a reception in the home of the Douglas Campbells.

The cannibals can't eat you if you have been formally presented, because that makes you their friend, and they regard their friends as relatives.

But the cannibals are no stranger than the tribe that traps floating islands. Those people wait until an island comes floating along, and then they catch it and tie it up. They plant a crop, harvest it, and finally set the island adrift once more, because the mosquitoes on floating islands are most annoying.

THE PIRATES

The restaurant boat *Rotarian* was scuttled by pirates. That's how she got to the bottom of the river, divers said yesterday, for the seacocks were open, and hardly anyone but pirates would have opened them.

The pirates, it seems, were out walking the plank one night when they crossed the Clark Street bridge. The head pirate said:

"My goodness, boys, that's the old *Rotarian*. They burned my steak there last night, and spilled soup on my shirt front. Let's scuttle her—send her down to Davy Jones's locker. You know."

"Let's!" cried the rest of the pirates.

And they all hurried down to John Crerar Library to read up on how ships are scuttled, in the encyclopaedia. The way that's most fun, they learned, is to open the seacocks on the bottom of the boat and let the water in.

So they did that.

Next morning there was an investigation. Ever since then, people have been raising the boat and then letting her slide back to the bottom of the river again.

Miles Devine, one of the owners, was finally ordered to move the *Rotarian* out of the river for that sort of thing. When the boat was pulled up to the surface yesterday, City Prosecutor Michael L. Rosina sent the divers to see who really sank her.

And imagine! They found out about the pirates.

HOSEA SELLS

All of his seventy-seven years Hosea Sells had been waiting to see Night Flower win this race—Night Flower, the greatest horse he had ever trained. Hosea Sells was going to retire, and they were all the greatest.

Last year it had been another horse. Next year it

would be another, for the weather-beaten old Hosea Sellses never retire.

When his green and gold colors flashed under the wire, and the name of the winner went up, those who thought Night Flower was an outsider would be asking who the owner was.

Then they'd discover that Hosea Sells was the owner. And trainer. Old-timers would recall Hosea Sells's surprises on many another track.

He was glad it would be Washington Park, for Hosea Sells, who called Waukegan home, gloried in his Chicago triumphs.

Now they were coming into the stretch. The horse he had brought back from Louisville was justifying his endless hours of training. Night Flower was moving up. Now he was fighting it out for first place. Now—

Hosea Sells's heart stopped beating. He did not see Night Flower crowded out by a quarter of a length. The excitement had been too great.

They were glad that Hosea Sells never doubted that Night Flower had won, when the old man was revived at the race track. That made it quite unnecessary to tell him before he died yesterday.

In those long-ago days, poetry and sometimes doggerel could get into the papers.

I had never heard of Cobus Kwaak, who wrote to the editor at Thanksgiving time, before the awesome winter of 1935–36. Mr. Kwaak said he was captain of the *Willie K,* flagship of the Blue Point, Long Island, oyster fleet.

For fifty-one years, he estimated, he had kept healthy by eating two dozen oysters a day except Sundays. And he wanted to say it would be a long, hard winter because the oysters were sleepy and fat, and that was a sure sign. (Boy, was he right! That was the winter the martinis froze in the glasses.) From that letter came this story:

158

COBUS KWAAK

Cobus Kwaak of the *Willie K* writes to the editor to say: Oysters are fat in Blue Point Bay. They're sleepy, too, these plump crustaceans, and so are most of their relations.

Willie K is an oyster smack. Cobus skippers this bivalve hack. Weather wisdom he doesn't lack. He gets his finest weather hunches from oysters that doze—and eat two lunches.

They mean a winter most severe, with days quite cold and evenings drear, says Cobus Kwaak, the weather seer. So heed this New York oyster man. He hopes you'll be as warm as you can.

THE BARBERS

"Egg shampoo? Haircut too?"

"If your story is really true."

"Barbers, hearken to this injunction. Trim beards, not prices, or cease to function. The Master Barbers Association complains of the price-cutting situation.

"Therefore I, Judge John McGoorty, decree that fifty instead of forty cents is the price of a good hair trim. Profits then will be rather slim.

"Egg shampoo, haircuts too, merit a proper revenue. I'll sign this order here and now, for Attorney Bailey Samelow."

The copyreaders said this one would be sung to the tune of "Reuben, Reuben":

EDWARD DUFFY

Edward, Edward, Edward Duffy, pinched a book of Gertrude Stein, off a State Street store's verse counter; couldn't understand a line. So he tried to sell it, but the man he tried to sell chanced to be the store's detective, who took Duffy to a cell.

Judge Eugene, Judge Eugene Holland, found that Duffy had done wrong, found he was a hobo, hobo; meted out a sentence long. Edward, Edward, Edward Duffy, didn't, didn't, didn't quail. He said stealing Gertrude's verses merits thirty days in jail.

Chicago Mayor William Hale Thompson, renowned for his threat to punch King George V in the snoot (CHICAGO TRIBUNE)

Queen Marie of Rumania, whose confidential chats at a society party were recorded by reporters posing as waiters (CHICAGO TRIBUNE)

Wilbur Glenn Voliva, religious leader who taught that the world is flat and
eating oysters is a sin because they have no feathers (CHICAGO TRIBUNE)

Texas Guinan, "Queen of the Night Clubs," who greeted guests with "Hello, Sucker" (CHICAGO TRIBUNE)

Bonnie Parker
of Bonnie and Clyde
(UNITED PRESS
INTERNATIONAL)

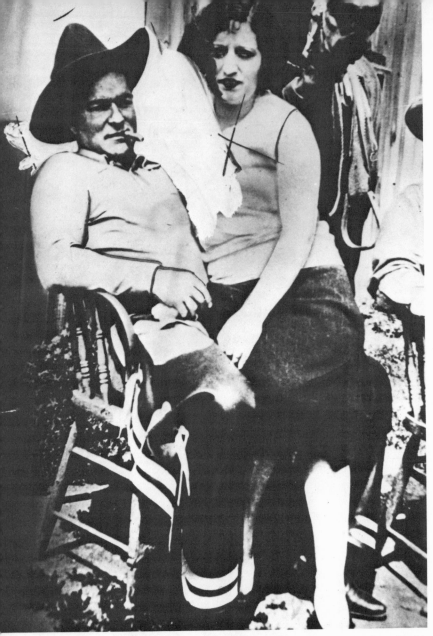

Diamond Louie Alterie, belatedly known as Two Gun Louie, with his wife (CHICAGO TRIBUNE)

Louise Rolfe, the "blonde alibi" of Machine Gun Jack McGurn in the St. Valentine's Day Massacre (CHICAGO TRIBUNE)

Smiling Sammie Samoots, the gangster who carried a sawed-off shotgun in a violin case (CHICAGO TRIBUNE)

St. Valentine's Day Massacre. Some of the seven victims on the floor after the shooting (CHICAGO TRIBUNE)

CHAPTER 17

George W. Barrett, the Kentucky feudist the government hanged in Indianapolis in 1936, was one of the singular personages in my life. By then, by government count, he had had several wives, two glass eyes, and an unfortunate mannerism of mistaking G-men for rival feudists. My first contact with George was when the City News Bureau reported that his lawyers were in Chicago asking the United States Circuit Court of Appeals to grant him a new trial.

Not that he hadn't killed the G-man, understand; George was never one to deceive, and after all, it would be a distinction to be the first man put to death under the new federal law making it a federal offense to kill a G-man. No, George did it, all right. His only complaint was that the government's witness shouldn't have told the jury that he had once said he'd like to kill himself and go up to heaven so that he could apologize to his mother for bumping her off the time she slapped one of his children. George had a hunch that that prejudiced the jury.

Well, the Court of Appeals said George would have to hang anyway. The federal law at that time didn't mention electric chairs. George became very angry indeed, then. He threatened to kill himself by eating his glass eye, but they took it away from him so that he wouldn't. He stalked up and down the floor of his cell, although competent doctors had said he never would be able to walk again because his knees had been practically shot out from under him in his battle with the G-men.

When he quieted down, though, he took to his wheelchair again. Phil Hanna, the Humane Hangman from Illinois, went down to make him comfortable and everything went off fine. Phil shook hands with him, told him he was the Humane Hangman, and offered him his choice of a black or white hood for the hanging. Phil said he was well qualified, having hanged no fewer than sixty-eight men before George. Then he gave George a surprise: He was going to use the very rope he had used on the celebrated George Berger of the Berger gang of Illinois, and eighteen other well-known murderers.

Phil explained that he began hanging criminals when Bryan was running for President, because he got so mad one time when he saw a hanging bungled by a nervous sheriff. As a matter of fact, Phil explained, he wasn't getting a dime for his work. George assured him that there weren't any hard feelings on his part and confided to Phil that he had a one-way ticket to heaven now. He could have killed himself even though they took away his glass eye, he said, because he always kept an extra one for emergencies, but he had given up the idea because of the sudden remembrance that he couldn't go to heaven if he committed suicide, and he didn't want to miss telling Mammy he was sorry.

George sent his middle-aged sister out to inspect the gallows. She reported that it was beyond reproach. And George, who at fifty-five had seen enough of life, went happily to his death that night, although not in his wheelchair. The Humane Hangman feared it might not go through the trap.

But Cheerio! All murderers don't hang, or fry either, as the police reporters call it when there's an electrocution. I talked to the lady who had her son-in-law killed, and the other lady who strangled him and cut off his legs.

Grim? Grisly? Not a bit. The mother-in-law, who fell in love with the man after her daughter died and then wanted him killed because she was losing him to a younger woman, was a welsher. She wept, and her chin trembled, as she tried to convince me that the killer she had hired had conceived the whole plot. "Anyway," she said with righteous indignation, "she was my best friend and she promised me we wouldn't be caught."

But the killer herself was no welsher. She denied nothing, smiled when the jury found her guilty, and observed, when I asked her whether she would rather go to prison or the electric chair, "Oh, I'm not fussy."

Whatever disadvantages there might have been in being a rewrite man on the *Her-Ex*, they were outweighed by the fact that it was the rewrite man who had the privilege of saving the copy from the City News Bureau. The Bureau's reports were news in the raw—precise reports of what happened, although generally they had to be cleaned up before they could be published in a family newspaper. Many a gem of purest ray serene was to be found in the Bureau's matter-of-fact paragraphs, which began, "Note to City Editor." More daring reporters, hopeful of being graduated to a job on one of the papers, sent through stories they knew couldn't be printed, which should have been notes to the city editor.

A Bureau reporter was listening when a widely-known industrialist who had had an operation for the transplant of monkey glands came to court on a speeding charge. The faithful newsman reported to the papers:

"——— ——— was overheard to tell his friend:

" 'Paul, I wish I had never done it. I'm right back there where I was before.' "

To another story of life as it is lived, the Bureau added: "Note to city editors: Miss ——— told Sullivan she got as

163

much as ten dollars, he said, but that two dollars is the regular price. XX."

Another Bureau story ended:

"Later, as Policeman —— stood in his pajamas and wiggled his toes in the openwork of his sandals, he confided his marital woes to an appreciative audience of his fellow policemen. Asked whether he intended to get a divorce, he said, 'I think I will. Was I mad? I ought to get one. Was I mad?' "

Note to city editors: Policeman —— said his wife and —— were having sexual intercourse when he interrupted them.

The story of a confessed arsonist responsible for half a dozen deaths in a Loop hotel ended:

"Note to city editors: Guerrieri said the threat that caused his confession was that he would be suspended by his testicles."

There was at that time a quaint theory that getting one's home bombed helped a candidate's chances for election. The better politicians generally arranged to have their homes slightly bombed just before election time. Sometimes the bombers misfired, as in the case of Health Commissioner Herman N. Bundesen, whose South Shore home was bombed when he wasn't running for anything. The stick was intended for a gangster neighbor.

Wags saw the possibilities at once and began sending imitation bombs to their friends. If the friend hadn't put in an order for a friendly bombing, he called the bomb squad in alarm and had the bomb soaked in water, just to be sure.

Faithfully, then, the Bureau would bulletin the editors:

"Note to city editors: The bomb, when opened, was found to contain horse manure."

CHAPTER 18

The gangland era in Chicago is regarded in these days as a grim period in our nation's history. It was. I know because I wrote most of the stories of the assassinations and massacres. Gangland chiefs were kidnapped right off the streets, or from their hideaways, and taken for Chicago's one-way ride, to be dumped, shot full of holes, in some lake or the forest preserve.

A lake, a small one, was the easiest way. The victim was weighted down with concrete blocks, so that his fate would never be known. A small quiet lake offered the least possibility that the concrete blocks would slip off.

But gangland wasn't all grim. Some of the gangsters were college graduates, disbarred from the practice of law or otherwise prevented from engaging in normal enterprise, who turned to crime. College professors, banned from education because of some spicy relationship with a girl student, turned to gangland. Competent accountants who had lost their licenses for turning out audits that were somewhat kinky became accountants for the gangs.

Scarface Al Capone opened soup kitchens during the Great Depression, and telephoned requests to me and other reporters not to mention it. He didn't mind being called the king of Chicago's gangland, but he didn't want to be known as a phony philanthropist.

Diamond Jim Colosimo, Diamond Lou Alterie, and Diamond Joe Esposito threw Christmas parties for needy children. If their restaurants chanced to be padlocked for violation of the Prohibition law, friendly federal judges removed the padlocks for the day of the party, and, if the gangsters' cars were all impounded, turned them loose so transportation for children who lived at a distance might be provided.

Kenesaw Mountain Landis, who as a federal judge outlawed from baseball the guilty in the White Sox scandal of 1919 and then became baseball's first commissioner, just winked when I asked him if he approved such goings-on. He said, however, that he'd never taken part in them himself.

Terrible Terry Druggan, an acquaintance but not a friend of mine, was a foremost member of the beerage. There were reports, which he vehemently denied, that he had been an English instructor in an Eastern college until he was fired for some youthful peccadillo.

Heaven knows why they called him Terrible Terry, although it was true that he never hesitated to have his enemies bumped off. He was a mild-mannered man who wore spectacles and collected rare books and etchings. He and his pal, Frankie Lake, were always getting sentenced to jail, not because they peddled beer but because they sold it at cut rates. The mobs didn't like that, and the judges went along. Sentenced, not jailed, was the word for it. Terrible Terry and Frankie bribed their jailers to let them out and spent their nights whooping it up in the speakeasies, getting back just in time for the morning check-in. They made their nocturnal trips in a limousine. Crime reporter Marion Gondeck had seen this car zip past him on several evenings. One night he speeded up to take a look and saw, as he had suspected, its occupants were Terrible Terry and Frankie. He hit Page One with his story.

When the six-day bicycle races gave way to the dance marathons, all gangland showed up around midnight. Feuds were forgotten at the marathons. Al Capone distributed $50 or $100 bills to girls who remained on their feet throughout the night, and he had nothing but smiles for his old enemies, the Morans, who were passing out tens and twenties.

Funerals were gangland social events of the Twenties. The going rate for a funeral for a long time was ten thousand dollars, and then gang lord Dean (Dion) O'Banion was shot to death in the flower shop he ran as a blind across the street from the Holy Name Cathedral. O'Banion was a sensitive fellow who couldn't just hang out a shingle reading "Dean O'Banion, boss of the O'Banion gang." Hence the flower shop facade.

O'Banion's friends and relatives raised the funeral ante to $12,500, and admirers sent flowers worth $50,000. From that time on, the sky was the limit, according to Austin O'Malley, who investigated things like that for the *Her-Ex.*

The vacant chair as a floral tribute came in with the assassination of Big Tim Murphy. His cost $2,500, the florist who made it told crime reporter Ted Todd. Two days later, the florist called Ted back. "Don't quote that price," the florist said. "Them white roses and scarlet carnations cost too much, and it takes a full day to arrange them. The florists' association is going to charge $3,000 for a vacant chair from now on." But the next vacant chair cost $3,500.

The neon crucifixes were yet to come, in an age when silver caskets were a tradition of gangland. Tommy Maloy, gangster czar of a motion picture operators' union, was honored with the first of the neon crucifixes. From that time on, anyone who had been anybody in the underworld had a neon crucifix.

The gangsters had a curious affinity for the newspaper folk, even those who fought them most ruthlessly. Big Tim Murphy was an ardent admirer of Pat Daugherty, the woman rewrite man. When he was planning to have an enemy taken for a ride, he used to visit Pat to establish an alibi for himself. He'd have the perfect alibi, because she'd have to swear in court that he was sitting beside her desk, shooting nothing but the breeze, when the one-way ride began. Pat, herself, could interview Capone whenever she chose.

Jakie Smith, star police reporter of the *Her-Ex,* interviewed Capone after every gangland shooting. He called Capone by Capone's favorite name, Al Brown, and was invited to all Capone's champagne dinners. Fred Pasley, who wrote the first biography of Capone, was always a welcome guest at Capone's soirees.

When the government was on the trail of Murray-the-Camel Humphreys, and he knew that he'd eventually have to surrender and go the federal penitentiary for not paying his income tax, like Capone, the man whose shoes he was wearing at the time, Murray went dodging around the city for days, trying to persuade crime reporter Maurice Roddy to take him in, surrender him, and claim credit for the capture of the current Public Enemy Number One.

City editor Harry Canfield was a pal of Big Tim Murphy, who also became a pal of mine. A few days before Big Tim was rubbed out by gangland guns, Canfield sent me out to ask about reports that he was organizing Chicago's maids and butlers into a union. Big Tim denied this, but sent me back with a gallon of red wine for myself and another for Canfield, whom he called "Canny."

Ashcan Pete was one of my favorite characters. He was a polished gentleman you might have taken for a bond salesman if he hadn't taken you for your bankroll first when you dropped into his Ashcan Club for a cocktail in Prohibition days. The Aiello gangsters liked him so much that they gave him a gun and a permit to shoot anyone anytime, Aiellos excepted. Ashcan Pete's marksmanship was superb, but his memory for faces was appalling. He was always shooting at one of the Capones and then discovering that it was an Aiello. So they took the gun away from him and gave him a speakeasy. He was in it when the police arrived one night. The torpedoes had just gone.

"Good shots!" he chuckled with his next-to-last chuckle. "Got me six times."

Not many reporters got to see an actual gang execution. It happened to Don Mathieson, though. He had run over for a quick one at a little basement place called the Tunnel in the after-midnight hours when in came Hymie-the-Slob.

Hymie was a collector for the Morans, and he had come to complain that the Tunnel didn't buy enough Moran beer. Nobody else was in the place when two Aiello mobsters burst in. Without a word they gunned Hymie down and then departed.

Don Mathieson knew exactly what to do to insure a scoop. He locked the front door and turned out the lights so that thirsty gentlemen who buzzed and said, "Joe sent me," would think the place closed. He then telephoned the city desk all the details of the murder.

After that he and the proprietor sat down to wait it out until the opposition paper had gone to press. Two o'clock came, and three, and four, and five and six. Then Don telephoned the police, too late for the opposition's final. The *Her-Ex* came out with a scoop, all because Don had known what to do.

Diamond Jim Colosimo was the most picturesque of gangland's celebrated triumvirate of diamond lovers—Diamond Jim, Diamond Joe Esposito, and Diamond Louis Alterie. Diamond Jim was always two steps ahead of the others. They kept their trousers up with belts, but Jim, being old-fashioned and comfort-loving as well as vain, wore suspenders as well. That gave him two extra diamond-studded buckles, and a lead nobody could overcome.

Diamond Jim began as a street sweeper and rose to be king of Chicago's old Levee district. When Prohibition came, he became the overlord of all the South Side beer-peddling business.

Wealth flowed in. Figures of influence clustered around him. A lover of music, he became a patron of the opera, and the great singers of the world were numbered among his friends. They came to his famed restaurant to eat and drink, or mingle with the notables of the underworld who were Diamond Jim's friends. And his romance with Dale Winter was one of the classics of the underworld.

Dale was a choir singer who rose, after Diamond Jim's assassination, to be the star of the musical comedy *Irene*. She was eighteen when a newspaper friend of Jim's brought her to him. He had heard her sing in church and told Jim she had what it took to be the star of his floor show.

It was love at first sight. She was slightly afraid of him, because of his awesome reputation in the underworld, but she was fascinated, too. And Diamond Jim was enthralled by her innocence and beauty. In no time at all she was the star of his café. He even persuaded his pal Enrico Caruso to give her an audition, but the great tenor's only comment was that she had a sweet voice.

Diamond Jim kicked out his wife and married Dale. Thereafter, she went shopping in his limousine. He showered her with diamonds. She persuaded him to learn to ride, and soon the Colosimos, in the most fashionable of riding togs, were familiar figures on the bridle paths. One day he took her shopping in the limousine and then returned to the restaurant. In the lobby, an unknown gunman shot him to death.

There were reports that his kinsman Johnny Torrio had ordered his execution. This was hard to believe, for Torrio had been his closest associate. Nevertheless, the police established that Torrio had telephoned him on the morning of the murder to tell Diamond Jim that two truckloads of hijacked liquor would be delivered that afternoon. Torrio had been most explicit about the time of the delivery, which chanced to be a few minutes before Jim was shot.

The funeral was one of Chicago's most spectacular. Diamond Jim went to his grave in an expensive bronze casket. Hundreds of Levee Democrats marched in the cortege, which stopped in front of the restaurant, festooned with crepe, while two bands played a funeral dirge. There were more than fifty pallbearers and honorary pallbearers, representing the Democratic Party machine and including judges and aldermen and notables of the underworld.

Bathhouse John uttered the prayers.

Diamond Jim's wealth had been estimated in the millions, but precious little money was found after his death. His wealth, except for the restaurant, might have been concealed in the safety deposit vaults of trusted relatives. None of it was in the name of his widow, who discovered that she really wasn't his widow after all, because Diamond Jim had married her without waiting for the time required by Illinois law between a divorce and a marriage. Jim's relatives gave her a few thousand dollars and kept the rest. She departed for New York and her stage career.

Diamond Louis Alterie was the most desperate gangster of them all, conversationally. He challenged the combined forces of Scarface Al Capone, Johnny Torrio, and the Genna brothers to shoot it out with him at the world's busiest corner, State and Madison streets, when they killed his buddy Dean O'Banion. But he never set any date. He was always terribly disappointed because he couldn't persuade the newspapers to call him Two-Gun Louie with any consistency. They pictured him, instead, as a sheik who wore diamonds and tried, rather unsuccessfully, to be tough.

He used to tell of the dire and dreadful things he was going to do to his old enemy, Captain John Stege of the police. But he merely blinked when Captain Stege caught him in the Frolics nightclub and slapped his face. Diamond Louie never was such a big shot after that. Disappointed, he returned to his ranch near Denver. There he amused himself by telegraphing his love, collect, to Captain Stege. Sam Blair, the heavyweight of the *Her-Ex*'s writing staff, duly recorded all of Diamond Louis's exploits.

When Diamond Louie eventually went back to Chicago, some old enemies caught up with him and assassinated him. And then, when it was too late for him to know it, the papers all referred to him as Two-Gun Louie.

Gangsters haven't any guts when they aren't standing behind a gun. Anybody will tell you that. The next time someone does, tell him about Schemer Drucci. Michigan Avenue's link bridge was going up one day to let a boat pass when Schemer was making a getaway from police. Seventy miles an hour, the speedometer read, and that bridge was going up, up, up, with the gap in the middle growing wider. Schemer drove up one side, gave his car the gas, and landed on the other. Fellows like that, of course, never live long. Schemer was getting tough with a cop one day, and the cop, remembering that Schemer wasn't called that because he was slow, decided that Schemer was about to begin shooting. So the cop began first.

Her-Ex photographers had guts, too. I'll never forget the day that Limpy Charlie Cleaver's mail robbery gang was shooting it out with the police in the prairie, where the bandits had stopped the train. Sol Davis was lying there between the robbers and the bluecoats, calmly taking pictures of both sides.

Then there was Hymie Paul, no shoes and no socks, his trousers rolled up to his hips, paddling into a Gold Coast hotel with three inches of mud on his bare feet, to get to a telephone the day the *Favorite* went down in Lake Michigan with an excursion load of kids. Sol Davis, after all, had only the bullets to look out for. Hymie had to face the dowagers and the outraged hotel staff.

The gangsters always stood together when their realm was threatened, although they might be privately the most venomous of enemies. This they did for Baby-Face Willie Doody, a gunman with a charming smile and a deadly forty-five. He was a droll fellow indeed, and gangland regarded him as extremely funny.

He didn't have an enemy in the whole underworld. Even his best friends, nevertheless, conceded that he must stand trial after he shot and killed a suburban police chief, for cop killing was something the gangs had to decry. But his friends never wavered in their support of this gunman who had killed his share of innocent citizens in holdups before he shot the police officer.

Covertly, Baby-Face Willie's pals established a defense fund for him. That is to say, they sold tickets to a testimonial to his good works, and while they didn't sign their names to the invitations they advised all and sundry to buy tickets—"or else." The money paid for Willie's lawyers, but it couldn't buy his innocence.

The jurors, dreading ever to meet Baby-Face Willie outside the courtroom, tried to insure their own hides by sentencing him to the electric chair. They worried aplenty when the judge reduced the sentence to life imprisonment, because they knew that Baby-Face was a charmer who would eventually get out on parole.

Dago Lawrence Mangano was one of gangland's better wisecrackers and a firm believer in gangland solidarity. When the 1931 Public Enemy ratings came out he learned with some chagrin that he was only Number Four.

"Us Public Enemies has gotta stick together," he told a reporter, Joe Hanson. And then he furnished bail for Number Twenty-Seven, who was under indictment for murder.

Gangland's sons, brothers, and brothers-in-law had the same problems as relatives in business and politics have now —getting out from the shadow of a better known relative.

Ralph Capone was the Number Two man of the Capone dynasty; yet he rarely made the front pages, and a gangster who couldn't get publicity was a dead duck. The only Capone the public knew about was Scarface Al. This worried Ralph and Big Brother Al until police reporter Maurice Roddy told them what to do: Put Ralph in charge of the Capones' bottle beer business, which wasn't much because most Capone beer was sold by the barrel.

The next time Ralph was arrested, Roddy dubbed him "Bottles Capone." The moniker stuck. In no time at all Bottles Capone was in all the papers.

Big Rabbit Connel's hutch was a brewery, and a cut-price one at that. Big Rabbit went around peddling beer at $35 a barrel when the Capones were getting $50. But his dumb bunny little brother, Little Rabbit, complained to me, meek soul that he was, that he never got any attention. The Capones, as you might suspect, went out hunting cottontails, and they shot Big Rabbit over on Chicago's Goose Island. Then all the papers said that Little Rabbit was taking over the gang and made him a town figure. He eventually got daring enough to become a patron of the opera. The Capones, for no reason that anybody could conjecture, left Little Rabbit alone. Perhaps they figured he'd go broke on his own, and he did.

Dingbat Oberta made it in the conventional way, not by marrying the boss's daughter, to be sure, but by marrying his widow. Big Tim Murphy's, that is.

Dingbat, like the man whose shoes he filled for a time, was one of the Dese, Dem, and Dose boys of the stockyards. Under the guidance of Big Tim himself, Dingbat had become one of the beer barons of Prohibition days.

He learned, although not from Big Tim, to ride a horse, to wear plus fours and play golf. Always a step ahead of the fashions, and the bullets—that was Dingbat. He didn't mind when his followers changed his name from John to Dingbat. A change of names, he always maintained, was good for a man. When he was campaigning for office in the Irish precincts, he usually changed his own name by inserting an apostrophe to make it read O'Berta and thereby convince the voters that he was a true son of the Auld Sod himself. Dingbat always wanted to be a state senator, but he never could get enough votes.

Like Big Tim, Dingbat always described himself as a graduate of "De Swimmin' School," which meant, in gangland parlance, the School of Hard Knocks. Yet Dingbat and Big Tim were always most flattered when the band played "On Wisconsin"—at their demand—when they strode to the speakers' table, fashionably late, at the testimonial dinners given by their political admirers. Dingbat would put away two dinners and tell the crowd that Big Tim was a swell feller indeed. Big Tim would put away three and assure them that Dingbat was a right guy who would get someplace if the police would ever let him alone.

Police who arrested them were required to ask their names, although all Chicago knew them both. Dingbat's customary answer was "George E. Q. Johnson." (Johnson was United States Attorney for Chicago.) Big Tim usually replied "Santa Claus."

After Big Tim was mowed down by enemies' machine guns, Dingbat consoled his peaches-and-cream widow, and eventually she married him. Dingbat was gangland's most solicitous bridegroom. He went to Henrici's restaurant in the Loop every morning, just as Big Tim had done, to bring home coffee cake for his bride's breakfast. Dingbat and his bride were a happy couple indeed. But gangland's guns spoke again, and she became gangland's most illustrious widow, with two assassinated gang chief husbands.

Sam Blair covered Dingbat's services, where she told him, "There never was so grand a wake." And Dingbat's secretary, who doubled as a bodyguard, confided, "The casket cost twenty-five grand."

CHAPTER 19

Cigar-smoking Bonnie Parker and her paramour, Clyde Barrow, have been pictured as members of Chicago's gangland, but they never made it into the big time. Both of them were too hot to remain around Chicago, and so they were consigned to the fringes. Gangster acquaintances of mine occasionally reported that Barrow had made contact with them, but the organized gangs wanted no part of the quick-shooting bandit, whom they regarded as a madman.

One of the stranger experiences of my life occurred one night, long before Bonnie and Clyde had become household names. I had gone down to a dance marathon in the old Coliseum on a tip that Aimee Semple McPherson and Texas Guinan would hold a peace parley in a box there.

No Aimee. No Tex. I slid over into a seat to watch the marathon. Presently the couple next to me departed, and I became aware of my nearest neighbor, a girl in a shabby coat who was smoking a cigar.

I moved over beside her.

"H'lo, Stranger," she said.

"What are doing in a place like this alone?" I asked.

"Watching the marathon, the same as you're doing."

I looked at the locket that dangled from her neck.

"B.P." I said, looking at the initials.

"For Bonnie Parker," she said, but the name didn't mean a thing to me. Bonnie and Clyde weren't known in Chicago at that time.

"Where from?" I asked.

"The Southwest," she said vaguely.

"Where are you staying?" I asked.

"At a hotel on Twenty-third, no, Twenty-second Street," she replied. "It's run by a fellow named Capone. My husband sent me up here to ask if we could get into his organization."

"You married?"

"Not really, but we're going to be. His name is Clyde."

I took her over to a little speak on Wabash Avenue, where I bought her a drink.

Then I called her a cab and hurried over to the office to see if the morgue had anything on Bonnie Parker. There was a picture of a girl of that name smoking a cigar, but the only information was that she had been arrested and released in Houston on a charge of bank robbery.

The term gang molls was coined by a Chicago reporter on a day when there were no gang shootings to make news. It was applied to gangsters' wives and sweethearts, and the title stuck, although it was most unfair.

Gangland's women, except for Bonnie Parker, were quite attractive and for the most part faithful to their men. The men, with the notable exception of John Dillinger, were faithful too. He kicked out Polly Hamilton for a sweetie known as The Lady in Red because she always wore red dresses. She was faithful up to a point, until the government threatened to deport her to her native Rumania unless she cooperated, whereupon she led Dillinger into the FBI ambush in which he was shot to death.

177

That was a story I didn't write, although I worked on it as a reporter because I was in the neighborhood.

Big Tim Murphy's marriage was a happy one indeed, as was his widow's subsequent marriage to his pal Dingbat Oberta. No divorce scandals ever marred the records of the Capones, the O'Donnells, the Morans, or the Aiellos.

The girls, having plenty of money to spend, bought their clothes in smart Michigan Avenue shops. They bought Sulka neckties for their affluent husbands, for the word was out that only a Sulka befitted a $250 suit. Husband-and-wife riding on the bridle paths was a must. The wives, doubtless, never had learned to ride at finishing schools, but they learned at riding academies and dressed as fashionably for their canters as did the ladies of the great families.

Under guidance from their women, the gangsters bought high-priced estates near the better suburbs or moved to South Shore or Oak Park. True, they lived under aliases. Occasionally their neighbors learned about them when one of the gangsters was involved in a shooting and the newspapers printed his address and true name. Then the women of the bridge club discovered that the well-dressed neighbor they all envied was really the wife of Frank McErlane, known as Chicago's cruelest mobster, or of some other gunman of equal importance.

White Diamond Betty Chambers got her name from the white diamonds she always wore. But the women of her clubs never suspected that she was anything but a wealthy housewife until she was found shot to death and identified.

Mrs. Margaret Smith was the soubriquet of a well-dressed beauty always seen at theatrical first nights. Gangland knew her as the Kiss of Death, for all a gangster had to do was have a date with her and he'd be found dead, the victim of one of her other admirers' bullets. The Kiss of Death never had anything to do with the killings, but her nickname made her social life unbearable.

Louise Rolfe, who won the name of the Blonde Alibi when

she gave an airtight alibi to Machine Gun Jack McGurn in a gang shooting, could have made the list of the nation's ten best-dressed women.

The kids were always a problem. When they were little they were sent to private schools. When they reached college age, they were sent to the best universities. All of them lived under assumed names, for they were always in danger of being kidnapped for ransom.

Some of the wives had genuine talent. The wife of the Little Man had been a newspaper reporter, and since the Little Man was so often away from home on his killing forays, she occupied her time writing for the detective story magazines. Her stuff sold, too, for she knew what crime was all about.

Ice Wagon Connors' wife earned an honest living at the most unusual job a gangster's wife could have had, as a woman policeman. The underworld didn't like that; it was disloyal and perhaps accounted for her husband's exalted airs. He was a good shot, but even his friends said he was a haughty fellow who treated them as if he were driving past on an ice wagon. Hence, his name. Eventually some enemy told the authorities who Mrs. Ice Wagon really was, and she lost her job.

Texas Guinan was the idol of the more frivolous wives. They'd go down to watch the Queen of the Nightclubs and tell themselves they could do just as good a job, if they had her reputation. Two of the girls actually made it in the movies. But they found Hollywood far less exciting than gangland and came back to Chicago.

The Charleston broke up one gangland marriage. Charleston dance contests were the rage in those days, and Dottie Dan's wife, Elaine, tired of being left alone at nights, went to a dancing school and discovered that she was a whiz at the Charleston. She entered a contest and won. When her picture appeared in the papers, a theatrical agent picked her up and sent her on a nationwide tour. When she returned in triumph, she told Dottie Dan she wasn't coming back to him. He was an indulgent husband and let her get away with it—temporarily. But he didn't mean it. He had her telephone tapped, and one evening when he learned she was going out he waited at her front door and shot her.

Next to the fabulous funerals in gangland's social scale, and equally fabulous, were its weddings. Gangsters who owned large estates lent them to fathers who didn't have estates big enough for the occasions.

The fathers tried to keep the plans for the weddings a secret, but the mothers of the brides always leaked the word to the newspapers' crime reporters. And so at the appointed hour, the reporters appeared. They were frisked, as a matter of routine, as were guests whose faces were not familiar to the armed guards. And presently the father would be pouring champagne for the very men who had proclaimed him a killer the week before.

The men came in afternoon clothes and the women in their most gorgeous dresses. Even though they knew the story would never appear in the society section, they hoped their pictures might find their way onto the back pages along with those of their notorious husbands.

The guests arrived in sleek limousines rented from undertakers. Bulletproof cars, because they were impossible to disguise, were left at home. It wouldn't do to let the classmates of the bridal couple become suspicious. The bride's identity was always protected. To avoid being tossed out, the photographers were required to agree not to photograph her face.

The bridal couple's parents and the guests all used the aliases that they used in everyday life. So there was no danger that sombody might be introduced as Machine Gun Jack or Scarface Al Capone.

The bridegroom, whether he was a college student or the heir apparent to a gangland kingdom, was immune from the photographers.

And so it was that the weddings, while spectacles in Chicago, went unnoticed by the young friends of the bridal couple. To them, the pictures were only reminders of a collection of gangsters—not the wedding they had attended.

CHAPTER 20

The characters in Chicago's underworld might have come out of a book, except that Jules Verne himself couldn't have invented them. There were the big-timers, like Al Capone himself, the Genna brothers, Machine Gun Jack McGurn, Golf Bag Sammie Hunt, Greasy Thumb Jake Guzik, and Umbrella Mike Boyle, a union racketeer who sat in a bar once a month with an open umbrella into which building contractors dropped envelopes filled with cash if they didn't want trouble with his electrical workers. The *Herald & Examiner* reported these activities, but they continued, for Umbrella Mike was immune to prosecution. After all, he argued, if the contractors wanted to shower him with gifts, there was nothing illegal about their generosity.

There were small-timers, too, all earning sumptuous livings from their gangster activities. We of the *Her-Ex* knew them all. One was Louie-the-Louse, as charming a fellow as you'd meet in any dark alley. He was Chicago's champion murder suspect. When Octavius Granady was shotgunned to death in the bloody

Twentieth Ward, Louis was arrested because arresting him for something like that was an established custom. When anyone was murdered in gangland, in fact, the first thing that occurred to the police was to round up Louis-the-Louse.

Years of experience in beating the rap had taught Louis that an airtight alibi was a better defense than innocence. If you had asked him where he was going to be on next Thursday night, he would have snapped, from force of habit, "You've got nothing on me. I'm going to be at my Aunt Susie's playing Flinch, and I'll have six witnesses to prove it. Ask my mouthpiece."

Lovin' Putty was everybody's pal, gangland's original gladhander. He slapped the police on the back, poured them a drink, laid a brotherly hand over their shoulders, and told them they were his friends, when some busybody police captain sent them over to ask if he ever permitted gambling in his gambling houses. He was so affectionate when he was in trouble that the title Lovin' Putty had been bestowed upon him by Harry Romanoff.

Naturally, the police couldn't arrest a fellow like that. A few thumps on the back, and a drink or two, and the officers forgot what they'd come in to ask. It wasn't until they were back at the station house, and the captain asked them what Lovin' Putty had told them, that they realized what a perfidious fellow he was. They got frowned upon and sent back to inquire again if Lovin' Putty ever permitted gambling in his gambling houses. And the same thing happened all over again. That went on for years and reporter Frank Brunton, later a public relations tycoon but then an expert on Lovin' Putty, reported that Lovin' Putty never did answer the question.

You began thinking of the better life after talking to Deacon Buckminster. If you were smoking a cigar, you looked shamefaced and tossed it away. You bought the lot he was selling at such a bargain, and next morning, when you were thinking about the better life again, you strolled over from your hotel to see it, although you knew it would be just where the man of the cloth said it would be. It was there, all right, but Lake Michigan was billowing over it, as the Deacon's exploits were related in a series by Jerry Heil.

The Deacon was a protégé of Yellow Kid Weil, for decades Chicago's most successful confidence man. The Yellow Kid had a long yellow, or actually saffron, beard, and his long hair was of the same hue. He wore faultlessly tailored suits and spats and looked to all the world like a banker of his day.

The Yellow Kid could sell anything from the Michigan Avenue bridge to the Hotel Sherman on short notice, but when he had a really big con game going he rented an office, had the name he was currently using lettered on the door, and moved in his library, as the story is told by one of his biographers, the late Ray Brennan.

The library was a collection of blank books, purporting to be the biography of whomever he was impersonating. The name on the cover could be changed by pasting a new one over the old one, and the books looked very impressive indeed.

The dignity was so thick that the suckers never thought of looking into the blank books. The Yellow Kid is estimated to have taken his victims for more than two million dollars, but he was in his seventies before he was ever sent to prison, and then not for long.

The Yellow Kid always freely admitted to being a con man but insisted that the man he was fleecing was out to fleece him. His philosophy, often stated in newspaper interviews, was:

"You don't get taken unless you have larceny in your heart."

Paddy the Bear and Paddy the Cub Ryan were father and son. You've seen bears lumbering along on their hind legs, flopping their front paws in the air as though they were going to start a fight if they didn't get their share of the peanuts. Well, Paddy the Bear was like that, which was why Romy gave him his name, the Paddy coming from that good old Irish name Patrick. He packed a gun in one of his paws, and it wasn't peanuts he was interested in. He was just a bum, always looking for a fight, until Prohibition came along.

Then Nuts Nolan told him he could get all the fighting he wanted, peddling beer, and get paid for it too. So Paddy the Bear and Nuts shot their way to bossdom of the old Valley gang, and their friends agreed that Paddy looked more like a bear every day. After Nuts was taken for a ride by a rival gang, Paddy became the unquestioned sole ruler of the Valleys and, mindful of the fate of Nuts, always sat with his back to the wall and a forty-five in his desk drawer, so that he'd be ready for anyone who came in the front door.

Overconfident, one day, he swaggered out to find his body-guards missing, and hurried back to discover that his gun was too. He was just sitting down to contemplate what had happened when his young son came in. Paddy gave him the money for a new suit and told him to get out fast, but there wasn't time. Wally the Runt burst in with a squad of executioners and took Paddy away for a ride before his son's very eyes. The son, Rik, told the killers he would get them when he grew up.

Nine years passed. The youngster celebrated his twenty-first birthday. That night Wally the Runt fell dead. The wonder was that he kept standing as long as he did, with the weight of all the bullets that were pumped into him at close range. Next day, the other executioners were systematically shot to death.

Gangland welcomed a new face and new name, conferred, as usual, by Romy—Paddy the Cub. The Cub moved into his father's old chair, took command of the gang, and, as his father before him had done, sat thenceforth with his back to the wall, so that he could see who was coming in.

Everyone thought that Dago Lawrence Mangano, gangland's number one wisecracker and advocate of the gangsters' sticking together, was the West Side manager for Al Capone. But Dago Lawrence insisted that he was only an athletic club manager, Patricia Daugherty's stories in the *Her-Ex* to the contrary notwithstanding. The athletic club that was his headquarters was a gambling joint and the police knew it, but they couldn't do anything about it because he had a court injunction forbidding them from bothering him.

The district police captain, Luke Garrick, was a resourceful fellow. He winked, fired one of his star detectives, and told him to go out and make a living in Dago Lawrence's elegant club. The detective got the idea, and the evidence against Dago Lawrence. Then he got his police job back.

Up to that point it was funny. But Captain Garrick's home was bombed and his wife died from the shock, as the paper's star crime reporter, Austin O'Malley, wrote. No one had any idea who would have done such a thing except the captain, who knew, but couldn't prove it.

When Jake-the-Barber Factor quit trimming beards on Halstead Street, he might have joined his brother, Max, and become, like Max, a cosmetics tycoon. Jake chose gangland instead, and after a somewhat undistinguished career in the underworld, he decided to make trimming Britishers his calling.

He sold them over $7 million worth of phony stocks and then decided to try something harder, like breaking the bank at Monte Carlo. That was easy, too, for Jake-the-Barber. He played chemin de fer with Edward VIII, who was then Prince of Wales, and could call the Prince by practically all of his numerous first names, until the British investors began demanding their money back. Jake returned to Chicago, and just as he was beginning to look like a cinch for extradition to England, he was "kidnapped" by the Touhy gang, to which he solemnly averred he paid $80,000 for being turned loose.

The underworld didn't buy that story but insisted that he had had himself kidnapped so that he could enlist the aid of the federal government, after the fashion of politicians who had themselves bombed at election time to call attention to their campaigns. The government, anyway, wouldn't let the English extradite him, because its interest at the time was locking up the Touhys for their gang crimes.

Jake was needed over here to help convict the Touhys, and he did it.

Austin O'Malley, the *Her-Ex*'s premier crime reporter and a student of Jake-the-Barber's career, always called attention to Jake's flamboyant neckties. They were intended, O'Malley said, to divert attention from his face. That way his victims could never identify him.

Dandy Jack was the playboy of the nightclubs. He went to the old Rendezvous one night to celebrate the birthday of that darling of gangland night life, the Kiss of Death, and promptly demanded a bowl of cracked ice, which he intended to toss down people's necks. As the waiters hesitated, he shot two of them dead. Maurice Roddy, our first reporter on the scene, found him trying to fatten up his day's average with a few policemen when the cops killed him, just as the cracked ice was coming up, in those days before ice came in cubes.

All of Gunner McPadden's experience as a gunner in the Navy didn't help him much when the shooting began in the Granada nightclub at a New Year's party. He and Stubby McGovern were dying at their table before they had a chance to get out their guns. They belonged to Spike O'Donnell's gang but some of Spike's enemies had seen them first. The shooting gave some University of Chicago students a thrill, because the Granada was their favorite dancing place. I hurried to the scene, and as an alumnus of the school pleaded with them to tell me what they had seen. They were as tight-lipped with me as with the police, and it wasn't long until the gunmen were roaming the streets again, ready for more killings.

Jesse-the-Goof was an overstuffed cowboy who came to Chicago with two forty-fives and a reputation as the bad man of Texas. They called him Jesse James down there, because he was so tough. Chicago's most desperate mail robbery gang thought he was the very man for their greatest job, the $2 million mail train robbery at Rondout, Illinois, a suburb of Chicago. So they imported him, with his guns and reputation. Jesse was pushing his guns against the engineer of the mail train when the gang discovered that he wasn't as tough in Chicago-land as he was in Texas.

As recounted by Austin O'Malley, the engineer, a blasé fellow who had been around, suggested that they might as well both have a smoke. "For heaven's sake," protested the Bad Man of Texas, "we don't dare light a match here. Somebody might see the light and turn me in."

The engineer refrained from slapping him down, because he thought Jesse-the-Goof was being funny; and the gang got the $2 million. But they knew that Jesse hadn't been kidding. They offered Jesse, their head man, $5,000 as his share and he took it. Thought it was very nice of them, indeed, for he hadn't the faintest idea how $5,000 compared to $2 million, except that five was bigger than two. The gang renamed Jesse James Jesse-the-Goof. Jesse was obviously too simple a fellow to be allowed to roam the streets with the secret of the mail robbery on his chest. They sent him back to Texas, where he was arrested. There, true to his name, he confessed. That sent the gang to the penitentiary. And Jesse too.

The St. Valentine's Day Massacre of 1929 was perhaps the world's most spectacular crime. Seven Chicago North-Siders, six of them major figures in the Bugs Moran gang, were lined up facing a wall and machine-gunned to death. One was a traditional figure, the innocent bystander, who happened along at the wrong time. Bugs himself, the primary target of the assassins, escaped because he became suspicious and didn't attend his scheduled meeting with his lieutenants.

Bugs had risen to be boss of what was originally the North Side gang, after his mentor, Dean O'Banion, was shot to death in his floral shop opposite Holy Name Cathedral. O'Banion had long been a relentless enemy of Capone, and Bugs continued the feud. He became increasingly defiant and contemptuous of Capone, and gangland realized that it wasn't big enough for both of them.

The Capones were believers in the first strike.

On the day before St. Valentine's day, Moran received a telephone call from a hijacker with whom he had frequently dealt and whom he trusted implicitly. The hijacker was offering a truckload of whisky hijacked in Detroit, at cut prices. Moran told him to deliver the liquor at the Moran warehouse on Chicago's North Side next morning, and promised to have a crew ready to unload it. Moran himself was to head the crew, among which were numbered some of his top lieutenants.

Seven men were already in the one-story warehouse when Bugs strolled over. He noticed a police car in front and, suspecting a trap, returned to his nearby hotel. With him was one of his gambling bosses, Teddy Newberry, who lived at the same hotel. On their way, they saw mobster Henry Gusenberg and warned him against going in.

The driver of the car, one of those long black touring models the Chicago police used in those days, was in a police uniform and cap and wore a police badge, according to the woman owner of a rooming house across the street. The man beside him in the front seat, she said, likewise wore a police uniform, cap, and badge.

The uniformed men alighted and entered the warehouse. The gangsters inside surmised that it was a routine police raid and offered no resistance when the newcomers drew revolvers and took command.

At that moment, three companions who had accompanied them in the back seat sprang out with machine guns and, authorities who later reconstructed the scene, ordered the gangsters to line up with their faces to the wall. Then the gunmen methodically sprayed their victims with machine-gun bullets and fired a round of shotgun slugs to insure that all the gangsters were dead.

It was all over in minutes. Residents of the flats in the neighborhood later reported that they had heard the gunfire, which they mistook for automobile backfires. Two of the neighbors were rooming house landladies. They told police that three mysterious strangers had rented second-floor-front rooms from them, insisting that their windows overlook the warehouse at 2122 North Clark Street.

The mysterious strangers disappeared after the massacre. The police believed that their task had been to report when Moran and his party arrived. The police adduced that the mysterious strangers were gangsters imported from Detroit, and that they didn't know that Moran and Al Weinshank, one of the victims, not only looked alike but dressed alike. When the spies saw Weinshank enter the warehouse, the police believed, they drew down shades to signal to Caponeites circling the block in cars that Moran had arrived.

According to this police theory, the machine gunners knew when they entered that Weinshank, a new member of the gang, was not Moran, but they dared not do anything but go ahead with their grim task.

The only victim to survive long enough to get to a hospital was Frank Gusenberg. He had gone to school with Clarence Sweeney, one of the first policemen on the scene.

At the hospital, Sweeney appealed to him to tell who the assassins were and explained to him that Gusenberg's brother, Peter, had died in the massacre.

But the police reported that Frank Gusenberg's only reply, before dying, was, "I ain't no copper."

The innocent bystander was Reinhardt Schwimmer, an eye doctor. A resident of the same hotel in which Moran lived said that Schwimmer had fallen under Moran's charm and frequently visited the warehouse to see what was going on. He visited just once too often.

The other victims of the mass execution were Moran's brother-in-law, James Clark; Adam Heyer, accountant for the Moran gang; and Johnny May, a one-time safe blower, who worked for the gang.

The outraged Chicago Association of Commerce offered a reward of $50,000 for the arrest and conviction of the executioners. The state attorney's office and the city council offered

$20,000 each. Interested Chicagoans added $10,000, bringing the reward money to $100,000.

But gangland silence is gangland silence. Bugs Moran flatly refused to name the hijacker who had put his men on the spot.

Everyone blamed Al Capone as the mastermind of the massacre plot. But at the moment the killings occurred he was in Miami, answering questions of the Dade County solicitor, Robert Taylor, about gangland operations.

Everyone blamed Machine Gun Jack McGurn as one of the actual executioners. But Louise Rolfe, whom the newspapers promptly dubbed the Blonde Alibi, swore that he had been with her in the Stevens Hotel in Chicago at the time. So did McGurn, and presently he was cited for perjury. He solved that problem by marrying Louise Rolfe on the theory that a wife cannot be forced to testify against her husband.

The mystery never was solved. Even for a $100,000 reward, those who might have known what went on were afraid to testify against Capone.

Fred "Killer" Burke was partially identified as one of the executioners. But he was already under charges of murdering a policeman in Michigan. Michigan refused to allow him to be extradited to Illinois and he was sentenced for murder in Michigan, where he died in prison.

All gangster stories have strange endings.

On St. Valentine's day, seven years after the massacre, enemies who blamed him for it shot McGurn to death and left beside his body a comic Valentine.